Date Due

STRATEGIC INTELLIGENCE
AND THE
SHAPE OF TOMORROW

FOUNDATION FOR FOREIGN AFFAIRS SERIES

STRATEGIC INTELLIGENCE AND THE SHAPE OF TOMORROW

William M. McGovern

Published in cooperation with
Foundation for Foreign Affairs, Inc.

HENRY REGNERY COMPANY
Chicago 1961

FOUNDATION FOR FOREIGN AFFAIRS SERIES, NUMBER 5

The Foundation for Foreign Affairs, 64 East Jackson Boulevard, Chicago 4, Illinois, is a non-profit corporation devoted to the promotion of a wider understanding of international relations—political, economic, and cultural. Books in the Foundation for Foreign Affairs Series are published in the interest of public information and debate. They represent the free expression of their authors and do not necessarily indicate the judgment and opinions of the Foundation.

FOREWORD

This little book deals with some of the problems connected with strategic intelligence. For the benefit of the ordinary civilian who may be ignorant of the term, a word should be said regarding *tactics* and *tactical intelligence*, on the one hand, and *strategy* and *strategic intelligence*, on the other.

Tactics is generally defined as the use which is made, or should be made, of armed units once they have come into contact with the enemy. Thus as regards the Navy, tactics deals with how a commander should employ his vessels when he first catches sight of the enemy's ships, or at least comes close enough to spot them on his radar or by aerial reconnaissance. With the Army, tactics begins when the enemy troops are so close at hand that an offensive or defensive plan must be prepared for immediate action.

Tactical intelligence is an attempt to find the number and composition of the units which the enemy has at the beginning of the engagement and how they are being maneuvered during the course of the battle. For the most part, the study of tactics and tactical intelligence can best be left to the professional military men, and hence it has been largely ignored in the present work.

Strategy, on the other hand, consists of long-term plans of action designed to secure long-term ends. On a lower

v

level, it deals with the conduct of a single campaign. On a higher level, it deals with the overall conduct of a war. Strategic plans deal with determining where our military forces should come into contact with the enemy so as to be in a favorable position to attack or defend.

It was a strategic decision (whether good or bad) which made the Allies launch an attack upon Africa before landing on the continent of Europe. It was a strategic decision which led the Americans to advance against Japan on a southern route, via New Guinea and the Philippines, rather than from the north, via the Aleutians, as was proposed by many officers in the early part of the war. It was a strategic decision which permitted General MacArthur to engage in a policy of "island hopping," by-passing many Japanese outposts while advancing ever closer to Japan.

Strategic intelligence acts in support of strategy by preparing estimates of the long-term capabilities and intentions of the enemy, his strength and weakness in resisting attack, and where he is likely to be most vulnerable. Strategy proper must, for the most part, be left to professional military men, but in the preparation of strategic intelligence, the estimates of civilian scholars have frequently proved to be of the greatest value. It was the climatologists and the meteorologists who convinced the Joint Chiefs of Staff that an attack on Japan via the Aleutians would be unwise. It was the students of raw materials who convinced the Joint Chiefs of Staff that the cutting off of Japan from bases in Southeast Asia would do the most to weaken her ability to carry on the war.

CONTENTS

I
STRATEGIC
INTELLIGENCE

1
Can Future Events Be Foretold?

WITH the conclusion of World War II and the establishment of the United Nations many persons looked forward to a long period of peace. This hope has proved illusory. Practically every year since 1945 has witnessed the rise of some world crisis which could easily lead to World War III.

At the present time the prospects for a long-enduring peace seem dimmer than ever. Crises in Poland and Hungary are followed by open warfare in the Near East. Feeling between Pakistan and India over Kashmir grows more bitter. There is increasing fear of renewed Communist aggression in Southeast Asia. Periodically, the Chinese Communists threaten to seize the coastal islands held by the Nationalists in Formosa, or even Formosa itself. In like manner, the Russian Communists periodically threaten to seize control over West Berlin.

The vast majority of Americans, whether men or women, old or young, are deeply concerned with the nature of the road which lies ahead. Most important of all the questions are—is it to be peace or war, and if war, is it to be a great world war or a series of "brush fire" wars popping up in different parts of the world, a series of campaigns like those in Korea, Vietnam, or

3

Egypt? And if war comes, will it result in victory or defeat for the free world?

I do not pretend to know the answers to these questions, nor am I acquainted with anyone else who is in a position to know them. Neither the leaders of the American and the British, on the one side, nor of the Russians and the Chinese, on the other, can solve all of these problems because much depends upon the attitudes of many other peoples in Europe, in Asia, and in Africa.

At the same time, I think that we can, by careful study, give partial answers. At least we can examine certain trends in international relations, certain forces operating in many different parts of the world, which throw light upon certain possible and even probable developments. To arrive at these conclusions it will be necessary to make use of a sound system of strategic intelligence, which may be defined as the study of the long-range capabilities and probable intentions of our actual and potential enemies.

In order to make clear some of the implications of this term I am forced to deal with certain autobiographical matters. For some time prior to World War II, I had held a commission in the Naval Reserve. It was a matter of no surprise, therefore, that a few days after Pearl Harbor I was called to active duty. In obedience to orders, I reported into Navy Headquarters in Washington, but it was some time before I knew what my assignment was to be. Like so many other Navy reservists, I was a "jack of all trades and master of none," so it was difficult for the authorities to decide what to do with me.

Before long, however, fortune smiled on me, and I was

assigned to a post which proved to be both stimulating and enjoyable. For the first time in United States history all branches of the armed forces were under the overall control of an organization known as the Joint Chiefs of Staff, which at that time consisted of Admiral Leahy, General Marshall, Admiral King, and General Arnold. This organization needed a small group of officers from all of the services under its immediate command; and I was lucky enough to be one of the men selected to serve on the staff of the Joint Chiefs of Staff. The members of this staff were of all ranks, both high and low. Needless to say, I was one of the lowest in rank, being little more than a commissioned office boy. But this did not prevent my pleasure at having an inside view of how war policy was being made.

I was assigned to work with the Joint Intelligence Committee (hereafter referred to as the J.I.C.). Most of the men working for this committee were representatives of the various armed services (Army, Air Corps, and Navy), but there were also men representing the State Department, the Office of Strategic Services, and the Board of Economic Warfare. It really was to be a joint enterprise. But most of us were new at the game and had a great deal to learn. I remember asking naïvely just what was the nature of the task assigned to us, and how stunned I was when told, "You are to draw up estimates of the capabilities and intentions of the enemy so that, on the basis of these estimates, the Joint Chiefs of Staff can prepare suitable war plans."

How was it possible, I wondered, for a small group of men, however talented, to sit in an office in Washing-

5

ton and make accurate estimates of what Germany, Italy, and Japan were capable of doing, and then out of several capabilities, to decide which plan of action they were most likely to put into operation? At first I seriously doubted that we would be able to carry out our task; but orders were orders, and we set to work with a will.

This is not the place to discuss in detail the failures and successes of the J.I.C. Suffice it to say, at first we were handicapped by the fact that we Americans had long neglected the task of building up suitable intelligence agencies capable of collecting and evaluating news regarding what was going on in enemy countries. In pre-war days the Navy frequently selected its second-rate officers, men likely to be "passed over" (i.e., not promoted), for work with the office of Naval Intelligence. The personnel of Army Intelligence (or G2) was not much better. The State Department had a number of men guilty of wishful thinking—men who knew what Germany, Italy, and Japan *ought* to do, but who gave little thought to what those countries were actually *going* to do.

In addition, there was a great deal of rivalry between the different services, and it was sometimes difficult to make each service give up all the information which was at its disposal, even though this information was, by order, to be given to the J.I.C. as the eyes and ears of the Joint Chiefs of Staff. Quite frequently I found that there was inadequate co-ordination between the central J.I.C. in Washington and the various intelligence staffs maintained by each theater commander. As a result, I frequently had to go on roving commissions to all of the theaters of operation in order to be certain that all of the intelligence available in the combat areas was made available to our Washington office and to the Joint War Plans Committee.

In consequence of this situation, at the beginning of the war we Americans were well behind the Germans, the Italians, and the Japanese with respect to the efficiency of our intelligence operations. We were also well behind the British. In fact, we frequently had to ask the British for their advice and assistance in solving some of our problems. As time went on, however, we improved a great deal, and by the time the war was over we had one of the best intelligence organizations in the world.

It must be remembered that even the best of intelligence organizations has its failures. The J.I.C. made a number of serious mistakes. Only ten days after it had firmly predicted that Japan would launch no attack on the Aleutian Islands, the Japanese seized Kiska and Attu, two of the most important of these islands. In the summer of 1944, the J.I.C. thought it very possible that the Germans would surrender in September of that year. I can recall a number of other errors, but I can recall a far greater number of successes.

After the fall of Greece and Crete, many persons in the armed services believed that the Germans would launch an attack on Syria. The J.I.C. flatly predicted that they would not do so—and it was right. At a time when many persons were predicting that the Germans would try to invade England, the J.I.C. stated that such an action was highly improbable. When many high officers thought that Hitler would capture Moscow and

7

Stalingrad and subsequently wreck the whole Russian military machine, the J.I.C. stated that it was very probable that the Germans would fail in these objectives. Again the J.I.C. was correct in predicting that the Japanese would not attack Siberia and would launch no big-scale attack on India. It correctly predicted that neither the Germans nor the Japanese would initiate chemical warfare.

At the end of 1945, I returned to civilian life and thought that my personal contact with intelligence work was at an end, but it has proved otherwise. On a great many occasions in the post-war years I have been asked to give lectures on intelligence problems before such institutions as the Army War College, the Navy War College, the Air War College, and the Armed Forces Staff College.* On other occasions I have had to furnish intelligence estimates to various Congressional committees.

Year after year, therefore, I have had to make a number of definite and somewhat detailed predictions. Here again I have sometimes been proved wrong, badly wrong, but on a great many more occasions I have been proved right—sometimes startlingly right. On one occasion I was asked to prepare a special report on the Far East for the Congressional Committee on Foreign Affairs. This report was printed in March, 1948. I remember one paragraph with especial interest. Speaking about Korea, I said:

* In this connection, it must be emphasized that neither the staffs nor the students of any of these schools are in any way responsible for the ideas expressed in this book. I, alone am responsible for them.

It must be borne in mind that if we withdraw our troops from the southern zone it is practically certain that the small but powerful and well organized Korean Communists will attempt to seize control over the whole peninsula. There has already emerged in North Korea a ruthless and self perpetuating Communist oligarchy which is fully prepared to extend its sway over the southern area. In the event of the withdrawal of American troops, it is very likely that the Russian forces would directly aid in carrying out this coup. Even if this were not the case the Communists should have little difficulty in forcibly seizing power, as the Russians have already organized a Communist indoctrinated "North Korean Peoples Army" while in the south the Americans have neglected to organize any native force capable of meeting invasion from the north.

In spite of this warning, the American troops were withdrawn, and in a little more than two years after this paragraph was written, my prophecy proved accurate, almost to the letter, except for the fact that not only the Russians but also the Chinese Communists took part in the effort to enslave South Korea.

9

2
Secret Intelligence

THE main purpose of this book is to show that a proper study of strategic intelligence can and does produce satisfactory results and that this study need not be confined to a chosen few but can be undertaken by any intelligent person who is willing to abandon wishful thinking and make a careful study of certain basic factors in the social, economic, political, and military activity of the various peoples of the world.

In the first place, it should be emphasized that a successful study of strategic intelligence need rely only to a very small extent upon secret, or covert, sources.

Spies and Counterspies

Many people still imagine that intelligence officers draw their conclusions largely from the reports of spies or secret agents. An intelligence officer is supposed to be good at getting into and out of disguises, hiding under beds, stealing secret documents, and making contact with incipient traitors who are willing to sell top-secret information at a price. This whole picture is a gross exaggeration.

Most countries do, indeed, have espionage and counterespionage agents who busily ply their trade. High military and other officials do sometimes sell or give valuable information to enemy agents. But for the most part, the information obtained from such sources tends to be of secondary importance. The only nation which has been signally successful at this type of intelligence has been Russia. Russia has unfortunately been able on several occasions to put agents or traitors in sensitive spots, using native Americans, Englishmen, Frenchmen, and other nationals who were secret converts to Communism and thus willing to sacrifice everything, including honor, for the greater glory of the Communist cause. It was in this way that many very important matters, including the secrets of the A and H bombs, became quickly known to the masters of the Kremlin.

But Russia is the exception in this matter. Neither Germany nor Italy was able to achieve any great success through secret agents. Both were uniformly surprised as regards the exact time and place of Allied attacks against them. A few German agents managed to get into England, but the information they were able to gather was of very little importance. Nearly all the agents whom the Germans landed in the United States were soon uncovered by the F.B.I. and executed.

Prior to the war the Japanese were rather good at exploiting secret sources. They were able to buy a few military secrets from disloyal Americans; and they also made use of a large number of espionage agents, with such good effect that they secured very accurate information concerning the disposition of our naval forces in the Pacific and were able to wreak disaster at Pearl Harbor. After this attack, however, Japanese sources of secret information almost came to an end. The Americans became alert to the dangers of both treachery and espionage, and hence after the initial success of Pearl Harbor, Japanese intelligence became very ineffective. The Japanese never learned anything about our war plans, and our major campaigns against them always came as a surprise.

The secret intelligence of England and France was fairly good and provided some interesting and valuable information, but it was of secondary rather than primary importance. The English and French secret intelligence was derived in large measure from contacts with various leaders of the resistance movements in the countries overrun by the Nazis and gave a general picture of conditions under German military occupation. Occasionally, some information came in which threw some light on the disposition of German troops in certain areas, but in no case did such information reveal the true nature of German war plans.

American secret intelligence was very poor at the beginning of the war but improved greatly as time went by, largely as the result of the initiative and brilliance shown by General William J. Donovan, the director of the Office of Strategic Services (O.S.S.). But, here again, much of the information received from Donovan's secret agents was important rather than decisive.

Allen Dulles, Donovan's chief agent in Switzerland and now head of the Central Intelligence Agency (C.I.A.), was sometimes able to send in some very interesting information based upon secret conversations with German officials who were so disgusted with the Nazi regime that they willingly, and without pay, divulged all they knew. But, for the most part, they did not know very much. We got a great deal of information about social and economic conditions in Germany, but very little else.

We were able to get advance information regarding the attempted assassination of Hitler in 1944, but actually this information did us very little good. On one occasion Dulles did send in some information which might have been of the greatest value. He got wind, in a general way, of a plan for military action which eventually led to the "Battle of the Bulge" in December, 1944. He managed to send this information back to Washington. Unfortunately, on this occasion the top military leaders dismissed the whole story as "fantastic," with the result that no countermeasures were taken and the Allies suffered a bad, even though temporary, defeat.

On other occasions, O.S.S. agents were able to get some very interesting information from certain officials in the Vatican. These officials were vigorously opposed to Nazism and Fascism and, entirely without the knowledge or consent of the Pope, gave to our agents some information which came in from various ecclesiastical circles in Italy and Germany. But, again, this information, while of use in understanding the general conditions in the enemy countries, was of little use in trying to predict enemy war plans.

General Donovan was also very energetic in sending American agents behind enemy lines. I got to know a good deal about this because I became well acquainted with General Donovan in the course of the war, especially during the latter part of the conflict after I had become his liaison officer with the Joint Chiefs of Staff organization. On several occasions I traveled with him to the theaters of operation and watched his organization parachute American agents behind the German lines in Northern Italy and behind the Japanese lines in China. It always gave me a thrill to see these brave men start out on their perilous undertaking.

Some of these agents were captured and executed, but a good number carried out their missions successfully. Equipped with walkie-talkie radios, they wandered around the countryside and sent back messages regarding what they themselves observed or what they learned from friendly members of the native resistance movements. Sometimes this information was extremely useful, but, generally speaking, more from the tactical than from the strategic point of view.

Since the terms "tactical" and "strategic" are likely to be confusing to non-military men, I feel that a word more of explanation and a few additional examples are necessary, even though the subject was briefly dealt with in the Foreword. One of our agents might get in the neighborhood of, say, Trieste Harbor and send back a message that five enemy ships were berthed in the eastern docks and three in the western docks. This was extremely valuable information if the Allied pilots stationed at Ancona were planning an air strike the next morning, and hence was of tactical importance. But by the time this message was coded, sent to Washington, decoded, and sent to the office of the J.I.C., it was of very little importance. By that time these vessels had all departed, and others might or might not have taken their place. It was only if the news threw light on how the enemy planned to use their long-term shipping lanes that the information became of strategic value.

In like manner, some of our agents, having found out by either direct or indirect means that during the course of the day a German division had been moved a mile east or two miles west, would radio this information back to the O.S.S. offices in Florence. This information was of great importance if an attack in force was planned for the next day, but it was of very little value by the time it was relayed back to Washington. What the Joint Chiefs of Staff organization wanted to know was, for instance, whether the Germans planned to withdraw twenty divisions from Russia to France or from France to Russia during the next six months. For the most part, our secret agents were not able to supply this type of information.

In dealing with the problem of secret agents, a word should be said about a small but very valuable group in the South and Southwest Pacific theaters. These were the so-called "Coast Watchers" organized by the Australians. Nearly all of the Coast Watchers were originally Australian or English civilians who were living in the Solomon Islands or in New Guinea at the outbreak of the war. Most of them were planters who had supervised a number of natives in the cultivation of palm or coconut groves. As the Japanese approached, many of these planters fled, but others were persuaded to remain in the jungles of the interior and spy upon Japanese activities.

In many cases the Coast Watchers were able to send back some very important information. Sometimes they made mistakes. Although they were all given commissions in the Australian navy, it took them some time to recognize the various types of naval vessels. They frequently confused cruisers and destroyers. Not infrequently from their jungle hideouts they would radio back the passing of a Japanese carrier, when in reality what they had seen was an American tanker or LST (landing craft). Nevertheless, they were of enormous value in being able to forewarn Allied Headquarters that the Japanese had sent a naval force or an air squadron against our positions.

One of the most interesting of my war experiences was the secret visits I was able to pay to some of these Coast Watchers in their hidden bases. They certainly showed magnificent courage in keeping on with their jobs, for they knew that they faced not only death but torture if they were captured, as several of them were. Still, most of the intelligence they secured was primarily tactical rather than strategic.

Communications and Code-Breaking

Another important means of receiving intelligence—a means normally inaccessible to the layman or the civilian —is through what may be called control of various types of communications.

A word should be said about the radar and sonar devices which were developed during the war and which greatly affected the outcome of the conflict. All of the armed forces, both Allied and enemy, experimented with such devices, but British and American engineers, working together, got well ahead of the enemy in this field. By means of radar our men were able to spot the approach of enemy vessels or enemy aircraft long before they were visible to the naked eye. They would continue to spot the position of such vessels or aircraft even when they were close at hand but, because of rain or fog, remained invisible.

Unfortunately, radar does not function below the surface of water, but the newly developed sonar was able to overcome this handicap in large measure. With sonar our destroyers were frequently able to spot the existence and the location of enemy submarines lurking far below the surface. Using this information, our ships or planes were in many cases able to destroy these hidden submarines by means of depth charges. In very large measure it was because of sonar that we were able to maintain control of the seas, an all-important factor in achieving ultimate victory.

It must be remembered, however, that the information received by radar and sonar is also essentially tactical rather than strategic in character. For this reason such information was seldom sent back to Washington for us to evaluate. All that we had to know was whether an enemy submarine had or had not been sunk. This information was essential when we tried to draw up estimates as to the total number of enemy submarines still in operation.

A constant check on enemy radio communications also rendered very useful service in the intelligence game. Even when such communications were in an unintelligible code, we were usually able to determine, in a general way, where such communications came from and from what other place other communications, presumably answers, came. We could also estimate the volume and the length of such messages. In this way our communications experts were frequently able to make an informed guess as to the movements of the main body of the Japanese fleet. It was only when this fleet maintained radio silence, as in the days immediately before Pearl Harbor, that we lost track of its position.

It is with some hesitation that I mention another major source of intelligence during the war, and that is the breakdown of enemy codes by cryptanalysis. For a long time this matter was such a top-secret affair that I felt forced to make no mention of it, and even now the matter must be handled with caution so as to reveal nothing except what is already public knowledge.

It would appear that Americans are rather gifted at cryptography and cryptanalysis. Towards the end of World War I, experts engaged by the State Department succeeded in cracking several foreign codes, including the one used by the Japanese diplomats in their dispatches to and from Tokyo. This accomplishment was of great value when we were negotiating with the Japanese at the time of the Washington Conference in 1922. The whole of this story has already been told by Herbert Yardley in his book *The American Black Chamber*.

When Henry L. Stimson became Secretary of State, he was horrified at this method of securing intelligence. To his way of thinking, it was ungentlemanly, analagous to hitting below the belt. In consequence, the "American Black Chamber" was abolished, and for several years we remained in blissful ignorance of alien plans and policies which would otherwise have been revealed in this way.

As the tension with Japan steadily mounted, the Navy felt that it had to take the matter in hand, and shortly before World War II, some men from the Office of Naval Intelligence were able to break one of the Japanese codes. In this way the Americans could intercept the instructions sent by Japan to her Ambassadors in Washington in the latter part of 1941. It was while reading one of these intercepts on the evening *before* Pearl Harbor that President Roosevelt exclaimed, "This means war." Unfortunately, at this time the Army and Navy commanders in Hawaii did not possess the key to the code, and they were not warned by Washington of the danger in time. It was one of the most tragic failures of intelligence in American history.

All of this was remedied after the outbreak of hostilities, and thereafter not only the intelligence personnel in Washington but also their counterparts in the various theaters of operation in the Pacific were kept fully abreast of all the information which came in from this source.

Even so, all was not clear sailing, and there was frequently great difficulty in interpreting the true meaning of the many confusing and fragmentary intercepts with which we had to work. I was necessarily let in on the "Great Secret" (which was given the code name of "Magic"), and I well remember the long hours I spent in trying to make sense out of some of the scattered, sometimes incoherent transcripts which came over my desk.

Sometimes we were led astray in trying to form conclusions. I remember that on one occasion an intercept spoke of sending fifty flasks of mercury from Saigon to Tokyo. We knew that Japan was badly in need of additional supplies of this metal and that if she had been able to discover a mercury mine in Indochina our picture of Japan's economic problems would have to be altered. By good fortune, a week or two later I was able to find out that the fifty flasks referred to came from the cargo of a confiscated Spanish ship and did not indicate a new permanent source of supply. But we very nearly fell into a serious error.

Sometimes, however, it was possible to draw definite and correct conclusions as to what the Japanese were doing or planning to do and act accordingly. I feel free to mention two significant occasions when this happened. Early in 1943, Tokyo sent a message to Japanese Headquarters in the South Pacific announcing that Admiral Yamamoto, commander-in-chief of the whole Japanese fleet, was flying down on an inspection tour and stated when and where he was to land. Admiral Halsey took advantage of this situation and sent some American aviators to give the Japanese Admiral "a warm reception." The Japanese were caught off guard; the plane carrying Yamamoto was shot down, and Yamamoto himself was killed. This was a serious blow to the Japanese war effort, as his successors in the post of commander-in-chief of the Japanese fleet were markedly inferior to Yamamoto with regard to strategic planning.

Of even greater importance was the aid which the

proper use of Magic gave to the American cause at the Battle of Midway. During the early part of 1942, especially after the Battle of the Coral Sea, most American officers were convinced that Japan's next major effort would again be directed at the Southwestern Pacific, near New Guinea and Australia. Just at this time a careful study of Japanese intercepts by some of our intelligence officers convinced them that Japan was planning a sneak or surprise attack on Midway.

They were able to "sell" Admiral Nimitz, commander of the Pacific Fleet, and his immediate subordinate, Admiral Spruance, on the soundness of this idea. Using every vessel and every airplane available, Spruance set out to catch the Japanese fleet in ambush, and to a very large extent he was successful. The Japanese were caught by surprise and lost many of their best aviators and four of their carriers. Though we did not know it at the time, this was the turning point of the Pacific war.

Interrogation of Prisoners

Brief mention should also be made of the information received through the interrogation of prisoners of war. In order to learn more about this subject, in the course of my numerous missions to the combat areas, I once visited a P.O.W. camp near Florence where German prisoners were being interrogated. I also spent several days at A.T.I.S. (Allied Translation and Interpreter Section), near Brisbane, Australia, where Colonel Mashbir and his staff interrogated Japanese prisoners. Incidentally, in both places I thought that a superb piece of work was being done.

Not content with observing how other persons were carrying on this work, on one occasion I had the opportunity of trying my own hand at the game. On a trip to New Guinea I found that the commander of a group of PT boats was anxious to find out the route which the Japanese transport barges were taking when bringing reinforcements to that area. I thought that if we could capture a Japanese soldier I might be able to dig out the information. But the trouble was to secure a live Japanese. Most Japanese refused to surrender, and when one did, the feeling between the Americans and the Japanese was so bitter at the front lines that the G.I.'s were apt to shoot the prisoner on the spot rather than bring him back for interrogation.

One time I was out with the PT boats, skirting the northern coast of New Guinea, when a Japanese barge was sighted and attacked. After a short but sharp struggle the barge was incapacitated and captured. I was among those who jumped on the deck of the barge when we approached its side, hoping in this way to get my prisoner. I soon saw that most of the Japanese had been killed outright, but there was one man who, though wounded, was still alive. I was very pleased at the prospect of having a prisoner at my disposal. Just at this time, however, the poor devil stirred. The skipper of the PT boat, who was standing nearby, thought that the Japanese was trying to get in a last shot at us and immediately shot him through the head with his .45. This meant that I had lost my prisoner.

A week or two later I had better luck. I was on a visit to an Army detachment south of Salamaua and decided to go out with one of the forward patrols. By accident we stumbled upon a small group of Japanese soldiers. Most of them were instantly killed by my companions, but one was only wounded. In the light of past experience, I immediately threw myself on top of him, my whole body shielding him from further attack. I was able to lead him back to our camp, which was a couple of miles away. As we approached the camp I was worried, lest my prisoner would be shot at, but these fears proved groundless. The psychological differences between the front-line trenches and a rear base are enormous. The prisoner was soon surrounded by soldiers, but they were filled more with curiosity than with hatred. One or two of them even handed the little Jap some chewing gum and candy.

I soon found that in most cases it is better to handle Japanese prisoners softly and indirectly instead of subjecting them to a barrage of questions of direct military import. It so happened that my prisoner was born in a small village near Kyoto. I had once lived in Kyoto for some time, and by a curious coincidence I was acquainted with the priest of the Buddhist temple where his family worshiped. This established a personal bond between us and I was soon able to make him talk about his boyhood and education. Then the discussion turned to his personal experiences in the army after he was conscripted. I soon found out about the army units with which he had been connected and then how these units had been transported from place to place. At the end of two hours I had all the information I wanted—without the prisoner ever becoming aware that this information was of military value.

Curiously enough, it was usually easier to get important information from Japanese prisoners than from German or Italian prisoners. The reason for this was that the German and Italian commanders were well aware that some of their men might be captured, and so the ordinary soldier was carefully briefed as to what he should and should not say in the event he was taken prisoner. They were informed that under the rules of war all they had to tell was their name, their rank, and their service serial number. Many Germans and Italians told that and nothing more.

The Japanese commander, on the other hand, dismissed completely any suggestion that his men would ever surrender, as it was part of the stern Japanese military code (*Bushido*) that a man should commit suicide rather than permit himself to be captured. As a matter of fact, the majority of the Japanese carried out the stern dictates of this code, a fact which accounted for the scarcity of Japanese prisoners. But the few who were captured were utterly unprepared on how to conduct themselves under interrogation and in many instances imparted military information without in the least knowing that they were doing so.

It must be stressed, however, that most of the information derived from prisoners of war is of tactical rather than strategic value. We might learn about what transportation routes were currently in use and something about the current "order of battle" (i.e., what divisions or regiments were in a given area at a given time), but the average prisoner knew nothing whatever of war plans, or even about the strategic problems which faced his commander. He had little to tell, even if he was disposed to talk.

Captured Enemy Documents

Another source of information which is sometimes of value is found in captured enemy documents. It would be very nice, of course, to capture the headquarters of an enemy general with his secret papers intact, but this is almost never done. However, some information can generally be acquired by a study of the letters and documents which lie scattered about even a simple outpost after its inhabitants have either been killed or forced to flee.

Here again, captured Japanese documents were frequently more revealing than similar documents left behind by Germans and Italians. The German and Italian commanders were well aware that the American army possessed a number of officers capable of reading their language and took care to see that most important documents were destroyed before they could fall into our hands. A great many Japanese appeared to be oblivious to the fact that the Americans also had a number of experts in the Japanese language and made little or no efforts to destroy notes and memoranda before abandoning their posts.

A good deal could be learned from a perusal of official

orders and records. On the bodies of dead Japanese soldiers would frequently be found letters, sometimes letters from their families back in Japan, sometimes letters which they themselves had written but had been unable to send off. Of especial interest and importance were the diaries kept by many of the Japanese officers and men. Our American commanders were well aware of the importance of diaries and prohibited them from being written.

Personally, I greatly regretted this order, as I was very anxious to keep a personal record of the many interesting persons and events which came within my ken. Not having been allowed to keep a diary, I am sometimes a little hazy about the exact time when certain events took place and about the names of some of the minor officials I met in the course of my military missions. But considering how much we learned from the captured Japanese diaries, I have come to the conclusion that the order prohibiting diaries was wise.

We were very anxious that the Japanese should not learn about the extensive use we made of their diaries, so the whole matter was kept a top secret during the war. Occasionally, however, a mistake was made. On one occasion the headquarters of the Southwest Pacific Command issued a statement regarding the barbaric treatment accorded some of our prisoners and cited as proof some information obtained from a captured diary. This threatened to dry up a valuable source of information. A special dispatch was immediately sent out from Washington, however, and the mistake was never made again. Fortunately, the Japanese overlooked the incident. Diaries continued to be written, captured, and used for intelligence purposes.

I cannot conclude this section without giving a word of tribute to many of the loyal *Nisei* (Americans of Japanese ancestry) who worked in this type of intelligence. We did have some ordinary Americans with a fluent knowledge of Japanese, but their number was small. Consequently, in many of the combat areas it was necessary to make use of second- and third-generation Japanese immigrants, coming, for the most part, from California or Hawaii.

They had a difficult task to perform. Had they been captured by the Japanese, they would have been tortured to death as traitors. In spite of their proved loyalty and the valuable work they were doing, they were frequently objects of suspicion by other Americans. Sometimes they were shot at by our troops simply by mistake. I remember that on several occasions some of these *Nisei* intelligence men asked me to escort them back from the shack in which they worked to their living quarters, lest they be taken for Japanese spies and killed by our sentries.

3
Economic
Intelligence

So FAR we have dealt almost exclusively with covert, or
secret, types of intelligence, which are normally available only to military personnel or to civilians in the employ of the armed forces. But I again wish to stress the
fact that this is only one phase of intelligence—and not
always the most important phase. It is hard to estimate
such matters mathematically, but I am inclined to believe
that in preparing a worth-while strategic estimate about
20 per cent of the basic information comes from secret
sources and about 80 per cent comes from overt, or open,
sources. I use the word "overt" to indicate those facts
which are available to anyone able to make use of a reasonably good reference library.

In preparing an intelligence estimate, many different
factors have to be taken into consideration, but three
factors are of especial importance. These are: (1) the
economic; (2) the ethnological; and (3) the ideological
factors.

General Economic Factors

Everyone who has made a study of modern warfare is
fully aware of the importance of the economic factor.

Warfare today is not so much between men as between machines, and the country which is able to turn out the best equipment is likely to win the war. I am convinced that the average German soldier and the average Japanese soldier were just as good as the average American G.I., as regards both intelligence and martial spirit. But the United States was bound to win because the Americans were able to outproduce all of their enemies. In many cases, quantity is even more important than quality.

As regards conventional warfare, the equipment (such as tanks and guns) turned out by the Germans was just as good as our own—sometimes better, but the Germans were not able to produce as much as the Americans and were doomed to defeat. The same was true to a very large extent of the Japanese. In some ways, especially in the latter part of the war, the quality of American equipment forged ahead of the Japanese. Thus our radar system became much better than that of the Japanese. With the coming of the B29's, our long-range bombers became greatly superior to those which the Japanese were able to produce. But at the beginning of hostilities most Japanese equipment was as good as our own, and in some cases was definitely better. Ship for ship, the Japanese battleships, carriers, cruisers, and destroyers were equal to our own. For many months the Japanese "Zero" fighter was better than anything we could put into the air. During the first half of the war, Japanese torpedoes were infinitely superior to ours.

But the Japanese were woefully handicapped by the amount of equipment they could turn out. During the war the Japanese could never produce more than twelve million tons of steel a year, while American steel production soared to over one hundred million tons annually. This in itself meant that Japan was inevitably doomed to defeat if the Americans were willing to fight to the bitter end.

A large part of the American fleet was wiped out at Pearl Harbor, but in the latter part of the war the American fleet was far, far larger than at the commencement of hostilities. The Japanese, on the other hand, were never able to produce adequate replacements for the losses of combat and commercial ships incurred in the course of hostilities. For many months the Americans lost as many carriers as the Japanese, but with the Americans, there were always two new carriers almost ready for combat use for each old carrier lost, while with the Japanese, the sinking of each old carrier meant a permanent loss to Japanese striking power.

When a man proposes to make an estimate of the capabilities and probable intentions of any country it is essential that he make a survey of that country's economic resources. This, in turn, requires that he make a study of three factors: (1) the number and quality of persons capable of taking part in industrial production (engineers, supervisors, skilled and unskilled labor, etc.); (2) the total number and quality of the factories which the country possesses (allowance must be made for the additional factories which might be constructed in a time of crisis); and (3) the total amount of certain basic strategic raw materials which the country has at its disposal.

In most cases the answers, or at least the approximate answers, to these problems are readily available to the investigator in yearbooks, technical handbooks, and in commercial and industrial magazines available at any good library. I know from personal experience that from these sources there was more to be learned about Germany's and Japan's fundamental strengths and weaknesses in the economic sphere than from our secret sources of information.

By means of a proper study of economic resources, the serious investigator should be able to make a reasonably accurate estimate of the total amount of steel the country in question should be able to produce or secure each year. This gives him a chance to estimate the total number of trucks, tanks, arms, and ships the country can turn out. The investigator should also be able to estimate the annual production of aluminum, and from this figure he can guess at the number of airplanes the country can manufacture. The investigator should be able to estimate the quantity of petroleum, oils, and lubricants (more technically, POL) the country will have at its disposal each year. This, in turn, means that he can estimate the scale on which the country can operate its trucks, tanks, airplanes, and ships.

I remember very well the hours the members of the J.I.C. spent in making estimates of Japan's production of ships. I sometimes wondered about the validity of our guesses, feeling that we might be hopelessly wrong. However, when the hostilities were over and we had captured the official Japanese records giving actual figures on such matters, I discovered that our estimates were quite close to the actual figures. My respect for the claims of economic intelligence went up greatly.

In order to estimate Japan's capabilities at any given time, we gave special attention to her ships, studying not only her combat vessels but also her merchant marine, for we knew that Japan could continue the war only as long as she was able to transport huge quantities of raw materials from Southeast Asia to Japan and send finished products to her troops scattered throughout the Pacific islands.

We calculated what Japan's total shipping was at the beginning of the war (including ships captured from us and from our allies). We then calculated the number of ships lost as the result of the action of our bombers and submarines. We next calculated the total number of ships which the Japanese could build each year. This gave us a picture of the total number of ships the Japanese could operate at any one time. By the latter part of 1943, it became clear to us that Japan was losing in the war of attrition. She was losing more than she was able to replace. We concluded that before long Japan would not have enough ships to keep her economy going. After the war we found that these estimates, also, were not far from reality.

Our major difficulty lay in correctly calculating Japan's losses. In the early months of hostilities, many of our aviators and some of our Navy men were guilty of wishful thinking. They thought that they had sunk a ship when they had only damaged it. We learned to be very skeptical of their claims. One of the most famous of these

ECONOMIC INTELLIGENCE

cases was the claim that we had sunk the *Haruna*. The *Haruna*, it will be remembered, was a Japanese battleship attacked by our aviators, one of whom lost his life in a last desperate attempt to sink the ship. His comrades thought that he had been successful.

This message was sent to Washington, and President Roosevelt, in a nationwide broadcast, stated exultantly that the *Haruna* had been destroyed. A few days later, using secret (cryptanalysis) sources of information, the staff of the J.I.C. became aware that the *Haruna* was very much afloat and was only slightly damaged. In fact, the *Haruna* was one of the last Japanese ships to be sunk. We therefore kept her on our secret list of extant combat vessels, but we had to be careful never to refer to her publicly, lest we appear guilty of showing disrespect to our Commander-in-Chief, who had claimed her destruction.

As time went on, however, our aviators learned to be more careful in their claims, though we continued, and rightly, to discount many of them. The Navy was much more cautious in such matters than the Air Corps, and submarine commanders had to bring back positive proof of destruction before their claims were accepted.

The Distribution of Raw Materials

I have already spoken of the importance of knowing the total amount of certain basic strategic materials available to the enemy. I should also like to lay especial emphasis upon the geographic distribution of such materials, both inside and outside enemy lines, for the study of this subject will give, in many cases, valuable clues to the enemy's war plans. Thus when the Germans invaded Russia, the staff of the J.I.C. correctly predicted that in addition to striking at Moscow, they would make a determined effort to capture the Caucasus and the area just north of the Caucasus. The Caucasus was, of course, of major importance because of its oil wells. If the Germans had been able to capture these wells, their own very tight petroleum situation would have been greatly eased. Even if they failed in this effort and had been able to capture the area to the north of the Caucasus, they could have stopped the flow of oil to the Russian armies in the north, greatly weakening the whole Russian position. This explains the strenuous effort to capture Stalingrad and the adjacent area.

The study of the distribution of raw materials proved even more important when the J.I.C. tried, in January, 1942, to make an estimate of Japan's probable war aims. Was it likely that Japan would attack Siberia—or India? Or would she be content with overrunning Southeast Asia? We who worked for the J.I.C. spent several hectic days of research to prepare this report, but I am still proud of its contents. We decided that Japan would probably *not* invade Siberia. Most probably she would undertake no major invasion of India but would attempt to seize Burma so as to cut off supplies sent through this area to the Nationalist Chinese. But, we concluded, Japan's major effort would be directed against Southeast Asia, largely because of the economic situation.

We listed the strategic raw materials needed to main-

34

tain Japan's expanded war economy and found that most of them were to be secured in Southeast Asia. For the production of steel, coal was needed, but Japan was almost self-sufficient as regarded coal. Not so with iron ore. Japan, we estimated, produced less than 40 per cent of her iron ore requirements, more than 60 per cent having to be imported from abroad. Where were these supplies? Northwest Malaya and the Philippines. Japan had to import nearly all of her chrome and manganese. From where? From the Philippines and Indonesia. Japan had to import about 90 per cent of her petroleum. From where? From the two islands of Sumatra and Borneo. Tin and rubber would come from Malaya. Nickel would come from the Celebes. Much-needed bauxite for the manufacture of aluminum would come from various parts of Indonesia, especially from the little island of Bintan. When we had almost finished our report, some of us remembered that Japan would be in great need of artificial fertilizer in order to increase her agricultural output and so we added the two little islands of Nauru and Ocean to our list of strategic areas because these two islands were a major source of phosphates.

We felt certain that if Japan could capture and hold Indochina, Malaya, the Philippines, and Indonesia she would be able to maintain her economy indefinitely and hence we gave these areas top priority on our list of regions which the Japanese would probably try to capture. But we also added New Guinea and the Solomon Islands to the list. These two areas were of little importance economically, but we were convinced that the Japanese would take them, or at least try to take them, so as

35

to use them as buffers or as advanced outposts protecting the more valuable Indonesia and the Philippines from Allied counterattacks.

In preparing our papers we made use of the distinction between Japan's "Inner" and "Outer" zones. The Inner Zone consisted of Japan proper, plus Formosa. The Outer Zone consisted of Southeast Asia. In a subsequent paper, when Japan had indeed conquered this area, we speculated that if it were possible to stop all transportation between the Inner and Outer zones, Japan would be forced to surrender. In other words, if and when American forces were able to seize a key center, such as Formosa, and establish a sea and air blockade of all Japanese commerce coming from or going to the south, Japan would be at the end of her tether.

This was a very sound idea, and early in 1944 the Joint Chiefs of Staff were prepared to act upon it. They adopted the plan of "island hopping," by-passing the large Japanese forces still stationed in Southeast Asia, with the aim of striking at Formosa in the latter part of the year. At General MacArthur's insistence, this plan was modified to the extent that the island of Luzon (Northern Philippines) was substituted for Formosa. In some ways, at least from the economic point of view, Formosa would have been better, as this island is close to the Chinese mainland, making it easier to blockade all north and south traffic. However, the capture of Luzon served almost as good a purpose, and when early in the next year Okinawa was captured by our forces, I knew that we had sealed off all economic contacts between Japan's Inner and Outer zones.

This convinced me that we had only to sit tight and wait for Japan's inevitable collapse. The Army "Brass" did not share this optimism and continued to prepare elaborate plans for the invasion of Japan proper. In the meantime, the atom bomb had been perfected and two such bombs were dropped on Japan. This undoubtedly hastened Japan's surrender, but I am still certain that Japan would have surrendered before long, even without an invasion of the main islands, without the atom bomb, and without Russian entrance into the Far East war.

The study of the geographic distribution of strategic raw materials is valuable, not only because it frequently throws light on probable enemy intentions, but also because it is a very useful aid in the preparation of our own war plans. In this connection, I remember that in the spring of 1942 the J.I.C. was ordered to prepare a special paper on "Vital Economic Areas," i.e., the areas which were vital to the support of America's economy. The Joint Chiefs of Staff were anxious to find out what the economic consequences would be if the enemy secured control of certain areas, such as India and the Near East, to which we still had access. It was obvious that our war plans would have to be modified if the study brought to light any startling weaknesses.

The paper was duly prepared and accepted, and I am sure that it proved useful. With the lapse of years, most of its facts and figures and even some of its general conclusions are completely out of date. If the advent of World War III appeared imminent, it would be necessary to prepare a much-revised report on the subject. I certainly do not propose to incorporate such a revision in this book, but it might be of interest to point out certain basic facts and conclusions.

In the first place, it is rather surprising how many strategic raw materials the United States must import in order to maintain its economy. Enormously rich in certain things, in other ways America is very much a have-not nation.

Take, for example, the materials which go to make up steel. We have plenty of coal, including coking coal, but we have exhausted so much of our iron ore that we shall have to rely in ever increasing amounts on imports from Canada and Venezuela to keep our blast furnaces in operation. Our domestic supplies of chrome and manganese are of such low grade that we can make only limited use of them. A large percentage has to be imported from abroad. Chrome can be picked up in a number of different places, but manganese presents a more difficult problem. Prior to the war a large percentage of our manganese came from Russia, but in view of the present tension between Russia and the United States, Russia must be ruled out as a safe source for our manganese. The other principal source of manganese is India, but because of India's neutralist sentiments, it is quite possible that she will decide at any moment to ban the export of this material to the United States. It is essential, therefore, that America be prepared to expand production in other areas where managanese ore is known to exist (e.g., Brazil and the Philippines).

Many other things might be mentioned. Normally we

import a great deal of copper from Chile. Nearly all of our tin comes either from Malaya or Bolivia. Our industrial diamonds come from Brazil or South Africa. During the war, nearly all of our bauxite for aluminum came from Guiana, but fortunately for us, since the war sizable deposits of bauxite have been discovered in Jamaica and in some of the other West Indian islands. It is not necessary to go on with the list, for it is obvious that unless America can retain access to a number of key areas, she cannot maintain her economy.

As we look at a map of the world it is interesting to note which areas are and which are not of great significance to us as sources of raw materials. Curiously enough, Western Europe ranks very low on the list. We do an enormous amount of trade with this area, but it is mostly manufactured goods that we import and very little in the way of strategic raw materials, apart from a little mercury, which we get from Spain. In like manner, North Africa and East Africa are relatively unimportant, while West Africa and South Africa, on the other hand, produce raw materials which are of vital significance.

It is somewhat surprising to find that as a source of strategic materials for us, India is far more important than China. We can, it is true, make use of Chinese antimony and tungsten, but there are ample supplies of these materials in other countries; hence a complete embargo of trade with China does not and will not have a serious effect upon our economy. India, on the other hand, is of importance not only for manganese, as already mentioned, but also as a major source of our mica. In addition, the nearby island of Ceylon supplies us with most of our graphite.

The fact that India provides us with most of our mica is due to a peculiar circumstance. Actually, Mexico and Brazil have ample supplies of mica, but they have never produced laborers capable of peeling or flaking mica, while India has. Incidentally, the flaking has to be done by specially trained children. A boy is "retired" when he reaches the age of approximately twenty because his fingers lose much of their deftness. We would no longer be dependent upon India if we could only import a few hundred of these child workers into the Western Hemisphere.

Fortunately for us, many of the badly needed raw materials are obtainable from the other countries of the Western Hemisphere. Canada and Mexico are of vital significance to us, as are some, but not all, South American countries. The materials supplied by the Guianas, Venezuela, Brazil, Bolivia, and Chile are extremely important, but other areas produce little or nothing we badly need to protect our economy. From the point of view of over-all military strategy, it is essential that we permit no South American country to fall into enemy hands, but merely as sources of strategic raw materials, Argentina, Uruguay, and Paraguay are unimportant. In like manner, in order to protect the Panama Canal, it is imperative that the enemy be kept out of Central America, but as regards raw materials, none of the Central American republics is of any significance. We would not starve if we had to forego the coffee and bananas imported from Guatemala and Costa Rica.

Strategic Targets

Economic intelligence is also of very great value in picking out targets for attack by our land, sea, and air forces. The actual selection of individual targets has more to do with tactics than with strategy and is a matter which should be left with local theater commanders, but a group of men charged with collecting strategic intelligence can perform an extremely useful task by pointing out how the destruction of certain *types* of targets would most weaken the enemy and by assigning the priorities of these various types.

As the Second World War progressed, it became obvious that the Germans were doing a rather good job in selecting their targets, and my co-workers and I felt that we had to do as well, if not better, than they. For example, the Germans realized that our whole airplane program depended upon the aluminum derived from the bauxite deposits in the Guianas. For this reason German submarines made special efforts to sink the ships bringing the precious bauxite to the United States. For a while they were eminently successful and sank an appalling number of our ships until new and improved anti-submarine tactics on our part made this task too hazardous. This fact inspired us to find out where the Japanese got most of their imported bauxite. When we found out that it was from Bintan and two or three other small islands in Indonesia, we turned this information over to the appropriate Navy officials—with gratifying results.

It was clear that the Germans, in their attacks on British shipping, had not disposed their submarines haphazardly but had placed them where it was demonstrated, by a careful study of the shipping lanes used by British ships, that the best results could be secured. Inspired by this fact, one of the subcommittees on which I served made a careful study of the shipping lanes used by the Japanese in their trade with Southeast Asia, giving special attention to the ports where the Japanese tankers were in the habit of getting their petroleum for transport back to Japan. I have been told that this information proved useful to both submariners and aviators.

Curiously enough, the Japanese were rather poor at submarine warfare. They had excellent submarines and first-class torpedoes, but they stuck to the old tradition that submarines should be used principally as a striking arm of a combined fleet or in tactical support of other combat vessels. For this reason they made very little use of submarines acting separately in attacks on our commercial shipping, even the shipping which brought much-needed supplies for our forces in the South and Southwest Pacific. Had they done so, our losses would have been much greater.

It was obvious that the Germans were making great use of expert target analysis in their bombing attacks on England. To be sure, they went in for a good deal of indiscriminate bombing in the London area, in the hope of terrifying the British into surrender, but they also made many attacks on carefully chosen industrial centers. On the whole, their choices were well made, except that for some reason they tended to spare the important factories around Oxford.

The British were also good at target analysis, though

they were apt to go in for area bombing rather than for attacks on specific factories. The Americans, on the other hand, made a specialty of "pin-point" bombing, choosing specific targets for attacks. For this reason our intelligence staffs made elaborate studies of the distribution and relative importance of Germany's industrial plants. I remember that special attention was paid to factories producing ball bearings and to the plants producing synthetic gasoline. Another favorite target was the oil refinery at Ploesti, Rumania, from which the Germans derived a good portion of their natural petroleum products. Unfortunately, the first attack upon this target was made without adequate preparation and from unsuitable bases, with the result that our bombers suffered heavy losses wihout inflicting much damage. Later attacks were more successful.

As a matter of fact, the task of destroying Ploesti should have been assigned to the Russians, as the target was very close to Russia, but the Russians were notoriously poor at strategic bombing all through the war. Just as the Japanese used their submarines chiefly for close support of their other combat vessels, so did the Russians use their airplanes mostly in close support of their armies and paid little attention to independent strategic attacks. The only important strategic bombing made from Russian airfields was carried out by American planes and American aviators, who were, for a while, permitted to make use of Russian bases. Undoubtedly, since the end of the war the Russians have made strenuous efforts to make up for their weakness, but I have the impression that the Americans are still superior in this regard.

43

In the last few years I have devoted considerable time to the problem of target analysis for use in the event of the outbreak of a major war between Russia and the United States. I have some fairly strong feelings about the priority which should be given to target objectives in the U.S.S.R. I also feel reasonably certain of some of the targets in the United States which the Russians would seek to attack. But this is not the time or the place to indulge in frank discussion of such matters.

The Limitations of Economic Intelligence

So far, I have emphasized the importance of economic factors. At the same time, it must always be borne in mind that these are not the only determining factors and that sometimes the economic factors are only of subordinate importance. Modern science has shown that Marx's doctrine of economic determinism—the idea that everything is governed by economic conditions—is completely fallacious. In many cases, men—and nations—are governed by non-rational caprice, by a desire to secure prestige or to vent spleen on a rival. When Mossadegh of Persia seized the oil refinery at Abadab, he was well aware that Persia would suffer economically, but it gave him a chance to humiliate the hated English. In like manner, when Nasser seized the Suez Canal, he knew that this action would cause him severe economic headaches. He did it in order to increase the prestige of his regime. In the years to come, we must be prepared to wit-

44

ness many similar actions, especially in Asia and Africa, because of the force of fanatical nationalism.

In this connection another important and widespread fallacy must be pointed out. It is frequently said that the United States must continue indefinitely to pour out billions of dollars to the less fortunate of "undeveloped" nations, lest the citizens of these countries turn to Communism. This is sheer nonsense. This is not the place to argue for or against the general principle of foreign aid. Personally, I feel that some foreign aid has not only been good but absolutely necessary to safeguard national security, while in other instances this aid has not only been wasted but has caused actual harm. But without going into this point further, let me say that it is certainly wrong to argue that the attiude of a people towards Communism is determined solely by its standard of living. The standard of living of the Pakistanis is quite as low as that of the Hindus, but the vast majority of the Pakistanis are vigorously anti-Communist, while the bulk of the Hindus have been at least united recently in general sympathy with the Communist nations. In like manner, the standard of living of the average Turk is very little higher than that of the average Arab, but most Turks are violently anti-Communist, while many Arabs, including the semi-prosperous middle classes, are sympathetic to Communism.

4
Ethnological Intelligence

ANOTHER very important means of securing strategic intelligence is through the study of what I call ethnological factors. By this I mean the study of the predominant characteristics of a people or ethnic group at any given time. There are many students of strategic intelligence who completely ignore these factors; others vigorously deny their very existence. But a long and careful study of this problem has fully convinced me that a study of this kind frequently tells us which nations are likely to be with us and which against us in a time of crisis. Likewise, on many occasions we can make a fairly accurate estimate of the fighting ability of a given people at a given time.

Predicting National Attitudes and Capabilities

As an illustration of what I mean, in 1938, even before the actual outbreak of hostilities, it was already clear that Germany, Italy, and Japan were a threat to the other peoples of the world and that at any moment they might initiate an aggressive war. It was also certain that the sympathies of the bulk of the American people would be with the victims of this aggression. When hostilities commenced in 1939, it seemed highly probable that eventually the Americans would be dragged into the conflict on the side of the English, French, and Chinese, justifiably or not.

At that time I was far from being an expert at strategic intelligence, but it was not difficult to predict that the Germans, as a whole, would fight brutally but well; that the Japanese would fight savagely, fanatically, but well; that many individual Italians would fight bravely but that the Italian army, as a whole, would not be a serious menace. When the Russians came into the war, I was convinced that they would fight savagely, with little regard for casualties, but would be better on defense than on offense. Generally speaking, these predictions turned out to be correct.

In 1947, when the British gave up their mandate over Palestine, many of my friends predicted that when the British were out of the way, the Arabs and the Jews would compose their differences and that some peaceful political compromise would develop. I felt certain that things would turn out very differently and that there would be a long period of savage and vindictive fighting between the two peoples. On this point I was correct. But I was completely wrong in my preliminary estimate of the outcome of this fighting.

Because of the fact that the Arabs enormously outnumbered the Israelis and the Jews in modern times had shown little aptitude for military affairs, I at first concluded that the Arab League would defeat Israel. Fortunately, before I had a chance to make a public pronouncement on the matter I had a long talk with my old

47

friend and former colleague Brigadier General Louis J. Fortier, USA (Ret.), one of my ablest mentors on the military side of strategic intelligence. He had come to have a high regard for the morale and the fighting spirit of the Israelis and a rather low regard for the fighting spirit of many of the Arabs, especially for the armed forces of Egypt.

As a result of the factors brought out by General Fortier, when I had to give a lecture on the subject, I rather cautiously predicted that the Israelis would probably be able to hold their own in the armed struggle. Further study of the problem convinced me of the fundamental soundness of Fortier's position, and in 1956, when Israel invaded Egypt, I was less cautious in my predictions that the Israelis would drive the Egyptian forces back. Even so, I was distinctly surprised at the overwhelming victory the Israeli army was able to achieve before United Nations intervention brought the conflict to an end.

In talking about ethnological factors, it is important to emphasize that we are dealing with ethnic groups as a whole and not with individual members of these groups. Some Germans, for example, are intelligent, some stupid; some are industrious, some lazy; some are courageous, some cowardly; some make excellent soldiers, some do not. The same thing is true of the Italians, the Turks, the Arabs, and all the other ethnic groups into which the world is divided. All that we can say is that at any given time the bulk of the soldiers may be good or bad soldiers.

I should like to emphasize the phrase "at any given time." This very phrase shows that ethnic character is not the same as racial character. Racial characteristics are purely biological, being transmitted by genes and chromosomes. In the absence of racial mixture, they tend to remain fairly constant over a long period of time. Thus the peasants of modern Egypt are racially very similar to their biological ancestors, the subjects of the ancient Pharaohs. Ethnic character, on the other hand, is formed by the complex of likes and dislikes, traditional and emotional motivations of a given people at given times, and tends to vary markedly from time to time.

In the seventh century A.D., the Arabs were superb fighters. Today they tend to be inferior fighters. In another century they may again be superb fighters. For the last thousand years the Jews have been notoriously lacking in military interest and ability. Today the Israeli soldiers are outstanding fighters. But in another century or two the martial abilities of the Israelis may have disappeared. The same is true of all the other ethnic groups.

When we try to prepare an estimate of the national character of a given people at a given time, it is necessary to bear in mind a number of conditioning factors: (1) race, real or imaginary, and the tensions which sometimes arise out of racial differences; (2) language and the affinities and differences between languages; and (3) religion and other traditional beliefs and attitudes. Two other factors tend to be of lesser significance: social culture and material culture. All of these factors go into the formation of national character, but at various times and places some of these factors are more important than others. Sometimes it is race and the tensions which arise

49

from racial differences. Sometimes it is language. Sometimes it is religion. Occasionally, social and material culture become matters of major significance.

Race

A discussion of race brings out a major paradox. As I
have already indicated, race, in the true biological sense
of the word, is of very little importance in the formation
and preservation of national characteristics. Yet it is also
true that the emotions aroused by racial similarities and
dissimilarities have a profound effect upon the political
and military attitudes of a given people.

Most popular statements made about race are complete nonsense. Such, for example, are the statements
made about the superiority or inferiority of a given race.
Many, but by no means all, anthropologists admit that
some of the scattered, more "primitive" races, such as the
aborigines of Australia, the Veddahs of Ceylon, and the
Bushmen of Africa are, or appear to be, inferior to the
higher races in that they are less capable of intellectual
effort, even with a favorable environment. On the other
hand, most, though not all, anthropologists think that it is
foolish to talk about the inferiority or superiority in dealing with the "higher" races, which include the vast majority of the human beings now living in the world.

There are a great many races and sub-races—authorities do not agree on the exact number. But practically
all anthropologists are agreed that there are five major
racial groups: (1) the Great Black Race, the Negroids;

(2) the Great White Race, the Caucazoids (the various types of Mongoloids are so differentiated that they must be listed as follows); (3) the Great Yellow Race, the North Mongoloids; (4) the Great Brown Race, the South Mongoloids; and (5) the Amerinds, the pre-Columbian aborigines of North and South America.

It is beyond dispute that within each of these racial groups some individuals are intelligent and some are stupid; some are artistic and some are not. The most that can be said is that the proportion of unusually intelligent or gifted persons is greater within one racial group than within another. But even this statement is open to serious doubt and is denied by some anthropologists.

To the student of strategic intelligence the matter is of little importance. Even if we accept the view that all of these five races are "equal," the fact remains that there is frequently tension and ill will when groups with widely different racial backgrounds come into close contact with one another. We may well say that racial prejudice is unjustified and even evil, but the fact remains that it exists. In many cases the study of these prejudices can tell us how a given people will probably act when it becomes involved, either politically or militarily, with other peoples of a different race.

We must admit that racial prejudice colors the lives and actions of many Caucazoids in the United States and in the Union of South Africa. We must also realize that racial prejudice is not confined to Caucazoids. There are many Chinese (North Mongoloids) resident in Southeast Asia, the home of the South Mongoloids, and in this area racial tension between the two groups is quite common. The feeling between the Negroes and Hindus in East Africa is usually bitter. Many North Mongoloids feel intense animosity against all Caucazoids, a fact which gives rise to occasional anti-American riots, even in such friendly countries as Japan and Formosa. The large and power Afro-Asiatic bloc in the United Nations is held together almost exclusively by a common dislike on the part of darker-skinned peoples for persons with a lighter skin. Taking account of this fact, we can frequently foretell how a nation like India will react in a diplomatic or military crisis.

One aspect of racial prejudice is worthy of special attention. If in a given area a racial minority exists but is very small, there is usually a fair amount of racial tolerance on both sides. However, as this minority becomes numerically larger, racial tension tends to increase rapidly. Prior to World War II most North Mongoloids (Chinese and Japanese) resident in the United States lived on the Pacific Coast, only a handful living east of the Rocky Mountains. This meant that there was very little prejudice against them in the East and, unfortunately, a great deal of prejudice against them in California.

Prior to World War I, most Negroes in America lived in the Southern states. This meant that racial tension was great in the South and relatively unimportant in the North. In the last few decades, however, large numbers of Negroes have migrated to the North, with the result that relations between the whites and the blacks in this area have greatly deteriorated. When the Supreme Court handed down its decision outlawing segregation in the public schools, it was easy to predict which states and which areas within states would react most violently to this order. It was, of course, those areas with the highest proportion of Negroes in the total population. In those areas and in those states where the Negroes numbered less than 12 per cent of the total population, the order evoked no protest.

The same general rule applies to the intensity of racial prejudice among the peoples of Asia. In the remote interior of Japan, China, or India, where only a handful of Caucazoids reside, very little racial dislike of them is evidenced. Racial antipathy is much more apparent in the coastal cities, such as Yokohama, Shanghai, and Calcutta, where the proportion of the resident Caucazoids is much higher.

The rule also applies to the relations between the North and South Mongoloids in Southeast Asia. In those areas where the Chinese settlers are few in number, the natives show very little racial antipathy. In those areas where the Chinese number 20 per cent or more of the population, racial prejudice is generally much more intense.

A word should be said about the relations between the members of the various sub-races. Each of the great racial groups (the blacks, the whites, and the yellows) breaks down into a number of sub-races. It is not necessary, in fact it is impossible, to list all of these sub-races, but by way of example we might mention that though practically all of the inhabitants of Western Europe are Caucazoids, most anthropologists subdivide them into the Nordic, Alpine, and Mediterranean sub-races.

The Nordics, to be found mostly in Northern Europe, tend to be tall, blond, blue eyed, and long headed. The Alpines, to be found mostly in Central Europe, are a little shorter than the Nordics, tend to have light-brown eyes, and are usually round headed. The Mediterraneans are long headed, like the Nordics, but are much shorter and tend to have dark hair and dark-brown eyes.

These differences do exist, but for the most part they are of very little importance for our present study because of the absence of strong antagonistic feelings among the members of these various sub-races. Contrary to Hitler's pronouncements, there is no serious evidence that any of these sub-races is superior or inferior to the others. The physical differences among them seldom have any influence on the construction of national frontiers or on the framing or modifying of national policies or national character. There has never been a widespread feeling that all the Nordics, or the Alpines, or the Mediterraneans should get together and form a single nation-state, though the Nazis played with the idea.

Northern Germany is predominantly Nordic, while Southern Germany is predominantly Alpine, but this difference did not prevent the development of a strong German nationalist movement backed by members of both sub-races. In like manner, Northern Italy is predominantly Alpine, while Southern Italy is predominantly Mediterranean, but this difference did not prevent the rise of a united Italy. All three sub-races are represented in France, but this did not hinder the rise of a strong French nationalist movement.

At the same time, these racial differences should not be completely ignored, since occasionally they do enter into the formation of sectional feelings and prejudices. All Germans want a unified Germany. Nevertheless, most North Germans tend to have a mild dislike of South Germans, and the South Germans frequently make disparaging remarks about the North Germans. In like manner, there is a good deal of friction between the North Italians and the South Italians. Much of this sectional feeling is due to economic, social, and cultural factors, but occasionally a rather vague awareness of sub-racial differences comes into the picture.

I first recognized this fact when I was inspecting O.S.S. operations in Italy during the war. General Donovan had recruited a number of Americans who were of Italian descent and who spoke perfect Italian to serve as secret agents behind the German lines in Italy. As long as these agents operated in Southern Italy, they were mostly very successful, but when they were parachuted into Northern Italy, they were markedly less successful in carrying out their work.

When I inquired into the matter, I found that most of these agents were of South Italian stock and were typical specimens of the Mediterranean sub-race. Thus they were able to wander around Southern Italy without attracting attention and were soon able to establish intimate contact with the native Italians. When, however, these same agents roamed around Northern Italy, they had a different, or "foreign," appearance and had a harder time establishing close contact with the inhabitants of this area. Several of them told me that many of the North Italians despised them because of their South Italian background.

Language

Quite as important as race is the language factor. Indeed, I am inclined to think that language is the most important of all the factors which go into the formation of national character.

If we hear people saying "We Germans" or "We Greeks" or "We Arabs," they mostly mean people who speak the same language, irrespective of sub-racial variations. In fact, the influence of language is so great that many persons tend to confuse race and language and talk about races when they really mean groups who speak the same language.

Thus I have heard many persons (including university professors) talk about the Slavic race, the Celtic race, and the Anglo-Saxon race. As a matter of fact, there is no Slavic race, no Celtic race, and no Anglo-Saxon race. There are merely persons who speak a Slavic language, a Celtic language, or English. Some Slavs are tall and blond, some are short and dark; some are long headed, some are round headed. The same is true of the Celts and the Anglo-Saxons. The "Slavic race" is therefore a figment of the imagination. But for our purpose an imaginary race is quite as important as a real race as long as people believe in it and are willing to fight for it. There is no Germanic race, but a great many people believed that there was. They believed, moreover, that all members of the Germanic race should be united in one great empire. This belief was one of the major causes of World War II.

Similar beliefs are behind many of the most serious tensions in international relations today and may well lead to new wars in the not too distant future. Take, for example, the case of Cyprus. The Greek-speaking inhabitants of Cyprus claim to be members of the Greek race, and hence argue that they should be united politically with the other members of this race. There is, of course, no Greek race but only persons, belonging to various subraces, who happen to speak Greek as their native language. About half of the Greeks are predominantly Alpine; the other half are predominantly Mediterranean. The racial composition of the Greeks is thus about the same as that of the Italians, but because of the difference in language, the Greeks and the Italians have little or no use for each other.

The vast majority of the Greek-speaking Cypriots are predominantly Mediterranean in race, but so are most Syrians, most Egyptians, and most Sicilians. As regards racial affinity, therefore, it would be just as reasonable to demand that Cyprus be annexed to Syria, or to Egypt, or to Italy, as to Greece. It is the language factor which leads to angry mobs for *Enosis,* or union with the Greek fatherland. The Turkish-speaking Cypriots have a slightly higher percentage of Alpine blood in their veins, but for the most part, it is impossible to tell the Greek and Turkish Cypriots apart as regards their physical appearance. It is the language factor which leads the two groups to hate one another.

The situation in Algeria is very similar. We frequently hear of the intense hatred which exists between the French and the Arab races. This is utter nonsense. There is, of course, intense hatred between the Arabic-speaking peoples and the French-speaking persons of Algeria, but this has little or nothing to do with race. The vast majority of the Arabic-speaking Algerians are predominantly Mediterranean in race, but so are large numbers of the French *colons*. In a great many cases, if you were to kidnap a man off the streets of Algiers, rush him to a Turkish bath, take his clothes off, shove a sock into his mouth so that he could not talk, and then call in an anthropologist to identify the group to which the man belonged, the anthropologist would have great difficulty in determining whether the victim of the kidnapping was a Frenchman or an Arab.

A great many people in the United States tend to think of the native inhabitants of North Africa as being partly or wholly Negroid. This belief has been fostered by no less a man than William Shakespeare, who represented his Othello, a Moor, or Moroccan, as being a Negro. Now Shakespeare was undoubtedly a very great poet and playwright, but he was a poor anthropologist. I have seen thousands of Moors, or Moroccans, and very few of them showed the slightest trace of Negroid blood. Actually, there is a smaller proportion of Negroes in Africa north of the Sahara than there is in the United States.

The vast majority of the inhabitants of North Africa

are predominantly Mediterranean in race, as are also the vast majority of the people inhabiting the northern shores of the Mediterranean Sea. Actually, the racial composition of Morocco, Algeria, and Tunisia is very little different from what it was at the time of Christ, when all of this area was an integral and contented part of the Roman Empire. It is a change in language (and in culture) which has brought about the antagonism between the peoples immediately to the north and to the south of the Mediterranean Sea.

Language also gives us insight into the real causes of some of the loves and hates of the various peoples who inhabit the Asiatic portion of the Near East. I refer to the differences between the Turks, the Persians, and the Arabs. Time and again I have heard the leaders of these peoples speak of the Turkish race, the Persian race, and the Arab race. In point of fact, however, there is very little racial difference between these various peoples. They are all members of the Caucazoid race. The original Turkish invaders of Anatolia may have been partly North Mongoloid in race, but through many centuries of intermarriage with the earlier inhabitants, the Mongoloid strain has completely died out. I remember wandering all over the interior of Turkey looking for persons with even a semi-Mongoloid appearance, but in vain.

Most Arabs and most Persians are predominantly Mediterranean as regards sub-race. In Turkey this race is also well represented, but from ancient times (the Hittite Empire), Anatolia has had many persons with round heads (as opposed to the Mediterranean long head) and with rather beaklike noses (the so-called

Semitic nose). The people are probably variants of the Alpine sub-race, but it has been customary to give them the name of Armenoids. This physical type is common not only among the Turkish-speaking inhabitants but also among the Greek- and Armenian-speaking inhabitants of Turkey.

It might be possible to assert that there is a slight racial difference between the Turks, on the one hand, and the Persians and Arabs, on the other. But even this would be an oversimplification. Not only are there many Mediterraneans in Turkey, but there are also many Armenoids in Persia, Northern Iraq, and Northern Syria. If one were to waylay and examine an average man walking on the streets of Damascus, it would be impossible, if his lips were well sealed, to judge whether the man was an Arab, a Turk, or a Persian.

But the Persian, the Turkish, and the Arabic languages do differ, and differ profoundly, from one another. Hence the three peoples think of themselves as being members of different races. In consequence, they tend to dislike one another.

Not only is the Persian language quite different from either Turkish or Arabic, but it belongs to a very different language family. Actually, Persian is a member of the Aryan, or Indo-European, language family. Hence it is distantly related to English; somewhat more closely to Latin and Greek. Not only is the whole grammatical structure of Persian similar to that of the Aryan languages of Europe, but there are also hundreds of words which bear obvious resemblance to those employed in the European languages. Thus the word for "father," which is *pater* in Latin, is *pitar* in Persian. Mother is *mater* in Latin and *matar* in Persian.

Because of this fact, Americans find it is much easier to learn Persian than the other two major languages in the Near East. In recent years I have sometimes had to help in the training of officers about to be sent out as members of various military missions abroad. I have always urged that those who are sent to Persia should make a serious effort to learn the Persian language, assuring them that in two years they should be able to acquire a fairly fluent knowledge.

Turkish is, for us, much more difficult because it is in no way related to English or to any other Indo-European language. It is usually classified as an Ural-Altaic language, which means that it is distantly related to Hungarian and Finnish, on the one hand, and to Mongolian, on the other. Many scholars believe that it is also distantly related to Japanese. Certainly its grammatical structure is similar to Japanese, as I know from personal experience. I was never in Turkey long enough to make it worth while to master Turkish. But I did find it useful to pick up enough to communicate with servants and tradespeople. It so happens that I have a fairly fluent knowledge of Japanese, having lived for some years in Japan as a boy. I soon found that if I thought in English while using such Turkish words as I knew, my Turkish was unintelligible, but if I thought in Japanese and put in Turkish words, people understood what I said. The fact that Turkish is so difficult for us to learn is definitely a handicap to our military effort, for the largest and most important of our military missions in the Near East is in

Turkey, and most communications with the Turks have to go through interpreters.

Arabic is in no way related either to the Indo-European or to the Ural-Altaic families. It is a Semitic language and hence is related to ancient Babylonian, Assyrian, and Phoenician. But since very few of our officers know anything of these languages, the task of learning Arabic is a difficult one for most of our service personnel. Arabic is also related to Hebrew, but an American who knows Hebrew is not likely to be popular with present-day Arabs. Even the pronunciation of many Arabic words is very difficult for an American.

I have a friend, an officer in the Air Force, who was sent out to the Near East in order to learn Arabic. I happened to run across him again after he had been studying for about a year and a half. I asked him how his Arabic studies were going. He shook his head sadly and remarked, "You know Arabic is not a language; it is a disease of the throat." A few minutes later he added, "Perhaps you have to live with a camel for five years to make some of the sounds the Arabs make."

The confusion between race and language in the Near East has important political and military consequences. So thoroughly do the peoples of the Near East dislike each other that the very fact that the Turks are *for* us means the Arabs will tend to be against us. If we were to win over the Arabs, the Turks might well become less pro-American in their attitude.

Another very important consequence is that some eminent Arab leaders, such as Colonel Nasser of Egypt, claim that since all Arabic-speaking people are members of one race, they must be united, by force if necessary, into one gigantic Arab empire, which would be one of the great nations of the world. This means, of course, that all of North Africa and all of the Arabic-speaking peoples of Asia would be united in one domain. As long as this thinking dominates the minds of some of the leading politicians in the Near East, there are bound to be serious complications in international relations. We must never forget that it was the attempt of Hitler to unite all of the German-speaking peoples into one great *Reich* which led to World War II.

Before we conclude our discussion of the Near East, a word should be said about the serious confusion of race and language which is to be found in Ethiopia, or Abyssinia. The Abyssinians are, of course, predominantly Negroid in race, but most of them think of themselves as being members of the (non-existent) Semitic race. This is due to the fact that the chief language of the country is Amharic, and Amharic is indeed a Semitic language, being fairly closely related to Hebrew and Arabic. Most Abyssinians go even further and claim that they are descended from King Solomon and the Queen of Sheba.

This idea is based on the story, recorded in the Old Testament (I Kings, Ch. 10), that the Queen of Sheba paid a visit to Jerusalem in the days of King Solomon. This is all that is recorded. There is no hint of any sexual union between them. The whole concept that the Abyssinians are descended from such a union is undoubtedly mythical, but that does not prevent it from shaping Abyssinian public opinion on world affairs.

Turning now from the Near East to the Far East, we find that there is similar confusion between race and language, with important consequences in the political and military spheres. We already know that the vast majority of the inhabitants of this area are members of the North Mongoloid race, but any development of a sense of racial solidarity is handicapped by linguistic differences. Of especial importance is the difference between Japanese and Chinese.

It is true that in historic times the Japanese have borrowed part of their system of writing from the Chinese. They have also incorporated thousands of Chinese words into their own language. But basically, the Japanese and Chinese languages have absolutely nothing in common. Chinese is related, very distantly, to Tibetan, to Burmese, and to Siamese. Japanese, on the other hand, is similar to, and in all probability is distantly related to, Mongolian, Turkish, Hungarian, and Finnish, but neither in grammar nor in sentence structure is there even a remote resemblance to Chinese.

Chinese, for example, like all the other Sinitic languages, is basically monosyllabic, while Japanese is basically polysyllabic. In Chinese, practically all root words consist of one syllable and one syllable only. Where a Chinese word appears to have two or more syllables, such a word can be broken down into two or more component parts, each of which has a meaning of its own. Thus the word *huoch'e,* which seemingly has two syllables, is really a compound of two words: *huo,* meaning "fire," and *ch'e,* meaning "carriage." In Japanese, on the other hand, most words consist of two, three, or four syllables which cannot be further broken down. To give a few examples, the Chinese word for a man (male) is *nan* (one syllable), while the Japanese word is *otoko* (three syllables). The Chinese word for strength is *li* (one syllable), while the Japanese word is *chikara* (three syllables). The Chinese word for heart is *hsin* (one syllable), while the Japanese word is *kokoro* (again three syllables).

There is also a vast difference between the grammatical structure of Chinese and Japanese. Japanese grammar is very different from that of English (or Latin), but Japanese does have an elaborate and complicated grammatical system. It has declensions and conjugations, regular and irregular verbs, a difference between past, present, and future tenses. In fact, in the written language there are more than ten ways to indicate the past tense, some of which cannot be adequately expressed in English. There is a difference between the active and the passive voices. Unlike Indo-European languages, Japanese *conjugates* its adjectives. Thus there is a past, present, and future of such words as "white" and "good."

It is possible that in remote, prehistoric times the Chinese language had a fairly well-developed grammatical structure, but in the course of centuries most of this structure has been lost and today Chinese makes use of very little grammar. A Chinese word is invariable and does not permit such changes as in the English *man, men* or go, *went.* The Chinese say "one man," "ten man." There is nothing corresponding to the nominative, dative, or accusative cases of the European languages. At the most, use is made of prepositions to indicate relations between objects.

The Chinese normally make no distinction between the past, the present, and the future in their use of words. Thus they say "Yesterday I go Shanghai," "Today I go Shanghai," and "Tomorrow I go Shanghai." If it is necessary to stress the time of an action, they make use of auxiliary words. Thus "I want go Shanghai" indicates that "I shall go to Shanghai some time in the future." "I go complete Shanghai" indicates that the act of going is over and done with.

I often think of the rough time our high school students have in trying to master the intricacies of French grammar. They must learn the difference between *passée définie* and *passée indéfinie,* the indicative and the subjective. They must learn the various conjugations of regular verbs and then learn that there are many irregular verbs. Would it not be easier to learn Chinese, which has no such distinctions? Not only are there no conjugations in Chinese, no regular and irregular verbs, but in addition we may say that there are really no verbs at all. A word in Chinese may serve, without change, as a noun, a verb, or an adjective, according to its context in the sentence.

It would appear that English is slowly following the path which Chinese took centuries ago. We have dropped most of the elaborate grammar of the old Anglo-Saxon language. In recent days there has been a marked tendency to drop the subjunctive (We tend more and more to say "If I am" rather than "If I be.") Every day we find an increasing use of the same word sometimes as a noun and sometimes as a verb. Thus "This is a book," but "I will book you a passage." "This is my hand," but "I hand you a parcel." To me it seems quite conceivable that in another thousand years, English will be as grammarless as Chinese is today.

Another great difference between the Japanese and Chinese languages is to be noted. This relates to pronunciation. Japanese is a very easy language to pronounce. There are no peculiar sounds which are difficult for an American to hear and imitate. With the aid of a few simple rules ("All consonants as in English, all vowels as in Italian.") it is possible for an American to pronounce Japanese words practically perfectly after a few hours' study. The only difficulty for an American is remembering that in Japanese there are no tones and no—or almost no—accents. There are, to be sure, almost no tones in the American form of the English language, but we do tend to use a rising tone when we ask a question. This is not done in Japanese, which is probably the most monotonic language in the world. We Americans nearly always stress one syllable in a word, while in Japanese each syllable is given almost equal stress. Thus we make a mistake when we say Yoko*ha*ma, Hiro*shi*ma, and Naga*sa*ki.

Chinese, on the other hand, is a very difficult language for a foreigner, especially for an American, to pronounce. There are many sounds which we find hard to imitate or even to indicate with our alphabet. Thus the word we transcribe by *shih* is something, but not exactly, like the *shir* in "shirt." The word which transcribes sometimes as *tse* and sometimes as *tzu* is really more like a *tz* with no vowel. The parts of words which we transcribe with a *j* are really halfway between an untrilled *r* and a French *j*. Thus the word transcribed *jen* is something, but not exactly, like the English word "run." Equally complicated is the fact that the Chinese *k* is halfway between our *k* and *g*; *t* is halfway between our *t* and *d*; *p* is halfway between our *p* and *b*.

To make matters worse, Chinese is a language in which tones play an all-important role. We might almost say that the Chinese sing, rather than speak, their language and that a single false note makes a sentence totally unintelligible. The Chinese tones do not, of course, correspond to the notes of our musical scale, but the difference between these tones is just as great as between our musical notes. To add to the complication, the number of tones varies in different parts of China. In Peking (North China), there are four tones; in Nanking (Central China), there are five; in Amoy dialect, spoken in Southeast China and in Formosa, there are seven. I am told that in Cantonese there are nine tones.

It is difficult to indicate the exact nature of the tones by means of the printed word alone, but with respect to the four tones of Pekingese, suffice it to say that the first tone is high level, the second is rising, the third tone is down and up, the fourth is falling. A false tone completely changes the meaning of a word. *Tao*, first tone, means a knife or sword; *tao*, third tone, means a road or wisdom; *tao*, fourth tone, means arrival.

It is easy to see how foreigners frequently get into trouble because of errors in tone. When I was a boy in

Formosa, a Scotch Presbyterian missionary had to be sent home to Scotland because of linguistic troubles. He was a zealous and learned man, but he always pronounced Chinese with a marked Scotch accent. Worse still, he could never keep his tones straight. On one occasion when he wanted to say "I want to save you," he made a tonal mistake and said "I want to kill you." No wonder the poor man had to depart!

Of great importance in this connection is that the Japanese have even greater difficulty in mastering the Chinese tones than do Europeans and Americans. Years ago, when I was studying Chinese at the Peking Language School, I met a number of other students of different nationalities. I noticed that the English were the quickest to learn the Chinese tones, then came the Americans, while the Japanese made a poor third. The English were the quickest because they are apt to make greater tonal differences in speaking their own language than do the Americans. The Japanese were the worst because of the completely atonal character of their own speech.

I have stressed the great difference between the Japanese and Chinese languages because of the serious effect it has upon the psychological character of the Japanese and Chinese peoples. Due in large measure to this linguistic difference, both peoples tend to dislike and despise one another. More to the point, if the Chinese at any one moment are pro-American, the Japanese tend to be anti-American. In like manner, if the Japanese are pro-American, the Chinese tend to become suspicious of us.

Before closing our section on language, it would be well to comment on one or two other linguistic peculiarities. It is important to note that many of the peoples of Southeast Asia, more specifically the inhabitants of Malaya, Indonesia, and the Philippines, speak dialects belonging to the Malayo-Polynesian language group. This means that these dialects have nothing whatever in common with either the Chinese or the Japanese language families. For this reason, even if the Chinese Communists do succeed in conquering the whole of Southeast Asia, they will have great difficulty in assimilating the natives of that area.

It is also significant that the languages of Northern and Southern India have nothing in common with one another. The languages of Northern India, such as Hindustani, Bengali, Gujarati, are all related to one another, and they are all, in turn, members of the Indo-European language group. Hindustani, therefore, is quite closely related to Persian and very distantly related to English. The peoples of Southern India, on the other hand, speak one or another of four languages (Tamil, Telugu, etc.) which are grouped together as members of the Dravidian language family, which is totally unrelated to the Indo-European languages.

A man from the southern city of Madras finds it just as difficult to learn Hindustani as to learn English. In point of fact, there are thousands of Madrasis who know English, while only a handful can converse in Hindustani. In the not far-distant future this linguistic cleavage may well cause serious political trouble.

In the first half of the twentieth century, common dislike of the British conquerors made the Indo-Europeans of the north and the Dravidians of the south cling together. This feeling also led to the creation of a single Indian state. But the Dravidians are already beginning to feel a certain resentment against their neighbors to the north. This resentment is aggravated by the plan of Jawaharlal Nehru and his followers to make Hindustani the sole official language of India in the near future. If, as is likely, this plan is followed by an attempt to compel the southerners to drop their own language and speak only Hindustani, civil war will probably break out. In fact, because of this linguistic cleavage, I am inclined to think that in the course of the next few decades Northern and Southern India will probably break into two separate states.

Religion

In many (though not in all) cases, religious beliefs and practices play an important role in molding national character and in promoting national likes and dislikes. It goes without saying that I am in favor of complete religious toleration, but in making intelligence estimates it is imperative that I take into account religious differences because in many instances they lead to political animosities and even to open and bitter warfare.

I have already referred to the fact that when the British abandoned Palestine to its fate the religious differences between the Jews and the Arabs led to a long period of violence. I must regretfully add that for the immediate future I foresee very little chance of reconciliation between these two peoples. In fact, I feel forced to predict that things are likely to go from bad to worse.

I wish it to be clearly understood that I am neither pro-Zionist nor anti-Zionist, neither pro-Arab nor anti-Arab. If I were a Jew, I would probably be an ardent pro-Zionist. If I were an Arab, I would probably be an ardent anti-Zionist. Being neither a Jew nor an Arab, I am concerned only with drawing up an estimate of what future developments are likely to be, and I am still convinced that no peaceful and satisfactory solution to the Israeli-Arab dispute is likely to be found for some time to come.

There are moderate Jews and there are moderate Arabs who would, and could, achieve a compromise if left to themselves. Unfortunately, in times of crisis the moderates of both sides are likely to be pushed aside in favor of extremists. Under the influence of extremists the Israelis will not be content with their present boundaries but will seek to re-establish the Empire of Solomon in all of its glory. This would entail the conquest of all of Palestine, of Transjordan (i.e., the land to the east of the Dead Sea), and probably also of the whole of the Sinai Peninsula. Under the influence of the extremists, the Arabs will demand the destruction of the state of Israel and the expulsion of every living Jew from Palestine.

Let us now turn to India. It will be remembered that in 1947 England withdrew from India, permitting the formation of the two new states of India proper, which is predominantly Hindu, and Pakistan, which is predominantly Mohammedan. At that time, many—in fact most —of my friends confidentially predicted that with the withdrawal of the British the relations between the Hindus and Mohammedans would improve. Some even made the absurd statement that the ill will between the followers of the two religions was largely due to British influence—that the British, pursuing the Machiavellian principle of *divide et impera* ("divide and rule"), had deliberately fostered bad feelings between the two groups. Being fairly well acquainted with India, I took a very different position. I knew that the hatred between the Hindus and Mohammedans was deep seated and of long duration and that it was the British troops who had kept the two groups from armed attack on one another.

I even bet one of my friends, a journalist, a dollar that in the course of the following year at least ten thousand persons would be killed in religious riots. I soon wished that I had been sure enough of my ground to bet a hundred dollars rather than one, because it soon became clear that I had not been sufficiently pessimistic in my predictions. Exact statistics are not and probably never will be available, but it is certain that several hundred thousand persons were killed in the fights between the Hindus and Mohammedans, many of them murdered in cold blood.

It should be noted that it is not possible to assign greater blame to the one group or the other. Hindus killed Mohammedans and Mohammedans killed Hindus with equal glee anytime a favorable opportunity presented itself. It should also be noted that we are far from having seen the end of the affair. Some efforts were made to transfer large groups of Hindus from Pakistan and large groups of Mohammedans from India, but even so, there still remain many Hindus in Pakistan and India still has a large Mohammedan minority. Feeling between the two groups remains bitter and tends to get worse rather than better. It is highly probable that in the course of the next few years bloody fighting between the two religious groups will again break out.

The close connection between religion and politics is not confined to Asia. We can witness many examples in Europe. Religious conflict is not the only cause, but it is one of the major factors behind the bitterness of feeling between the Irish (or, rather, the South Irish) and the English. It is certainly not the result of a natural tension felt between Celts and Anglo-Saxons. The Welsh are just as Celtic as the Irish, but because the Welsh and the English are both Protestant, the two peoples get along fairly well. Political and economic injury (real or imaginary) inflicted by the English on the Irish in times past has something to do with the feelings of the Irish towards the English. But most of these injuries would long since have been forgotten had the Irish and the English shared a common religion.

At the same time, the fact that Northern Ireland is predominantly Protestant means that the inhabitants of this area are determined not to be absorbed into the Republic of Eire, largely because the latter is predominantly Catholic. It can confidently be predicted that for some time to come the union of Southern and Northern Ireland could only be accomplished by the use of force.

A study of religious convictions also helps us to estimate the present and future status of Poland. As is well known, Poland was—and still is—an area in which the bulk of the population shows an extreme devotion to the Roman Catholic church. The Catholicism of Poland is in contrast to the Lutheranism of Prussia, its nearest neighbor to the west. The Poles and the Prussians are separated not only by language but also by religion, which helps to explain the cordial dislike commonly existing between the two peoples.

The Catholicism of Poland also helps to explain the bitterness of feeling between the Poles and the Russians, their neighbors to the east. Both the Poles and the Russians are Slavs. The Polish and Russian languages are very similar. It would seem, therefore, that the Russians would find it fairly easy to assimilate the Poles. But this is not the case. The Russians (when not atheists) are members of the Russian Orthodox church, in close communion with the Greek Orthodox church. The basic culture of Russia is derived from Byzantium rather than Rome. The Poles, on the other hand, are not only Roman Catholic, but their basic culture is derived from Rome and Western Europe. For this reason we can confidently predict that the Poles will remain unruly subjects of the Russians, that they will continue to hate the Russians, and that they will break away from Russian control whenever they have a favorable opportunity.

In preparing intelligence estimates, it would be well to bear in mind that some religions are "tough" and some are "tender" in their relations with secular authorities. It must be emphasized that I am not trying to imply that one Christian denomination is true and the other false or that one sect is superior or inferior to the others. It is, however, important to predict whether a given ecclesiastical organization will or will not be stubborn in its resistance to the assumption of arbitrary and dictatorial power by the temporal ruler of the state.

In general it may be said that the Eastern Orthodox churches tend to be "tender," while the Roman Catholic church tends to be "tough." This is the result of difference in historical background. Throughout the Middle Ages the Patriarch of Byzantium, offical head of the Greek church, lived in close proximity to the Emperor of the East Roman Empire and was rigidly controlled by him. If the Patriarch opposed the Emperor, he was likely to be deposed, or even decapitated. In later times, when the Russians adopted the Greek form of Christianity, a similar relationship developed between the Patriarch of Moscow and the Czar of Russia. Throughout its history the Russian church was in complete subjection to the secular authorities. Neither the members of the higher ecclesiastical hierarchy nor the simple parish priests ever dreamed of telling their followers to resist the demands of the state.

Curiously enough, a rather similar arrangement continues to exist today, even though the Czars have been overthrown and have been replaced by the leaders of the Communists. These leaders are, of course, all violent atheists, but they realize the value of making use of the ecclesiastical hierarchy for their own ends. So patriarchs and bishops continue to be appointed and to carry on their ecclesiastical functions. It is certain that these persons are not atheists, nor are they disciples of Marx and Lenin. They may well pray for the dissolution of the Communist party, but they will never urge their fol-

ETHNOLOGICAL INTELLIGENCE

lowers to engage in active or even passive resistance to the orders sent out by the Kremlin.

In the West a very different tradition developed. After the early collapse of the West Roman Empire, the bishops of Rome had no real temporal superior for several centuries and hence were able to develop a sense of proud independence. With the establishment of the Germanic empire, known as the Holy Roman Empire, there arose frequent conflicts between the popes and the emperors, but in these conflicts the popes were quite frequently the victors. The Catholic clergy, both high and low, continued to preach that when there was a conflict between the law of man and the law of God (as interpreted by the Church), true Christians were bound to reject the former and obey the latter.

This attitude has persisted into modern times. It is not, therefore, surprising that among the prominent critics of the Nazi dictatorship in Germany were such Catholic leaders as Cardinal Paulhaber. For this same reason I was quite prepared to witness the rise of such men as Cardinal Stepinac in Yugoslavia, Cardinal Mindzenty in Hungary, and Cardinal Wyshinsky in Poland as stubborn spokesmen against Communist dictatorship.

In the future, Communist tyranny may well provoke rebellion in Bulgaria, in Rumania, and even in Russia herself (all three Eastern Orthodox countries), but it is unlikely that the clergy will play an important role in such rebellions. In those countries, however, where Roman Catholics form a large section of the population, such as Hungary, Czechoslovakia, and Poland, some, at least, of the Catholic clergy will play a significant part in encouraging underground resistance to Communist totalitarianism.

Social and Material Culture

We turn now to a consideration of some of the features of social and material culture. The discussion of these problems must necessarily be brief and sketchy, primarily because the space alloted to us does not permit a detailed examination of the subject and also because neither social nor material culture plays as important a role in political and military affairs as does race, language, or religion.

Nevertheless, it cannot be doubted that the social culture of a given people at a given time has a great deal of influence in the formation of national character. For this reason the student of strategic intelligence will always give some consideration to the social, economic, and political traditions and institutions of a nation he is studying. He will want to know whether the people are literate or illiterate. (Illiterates tend to make poor soldiers.) He will want to know how much social mobility there is in the nation, whether outstanding young men of the "lower orders" can rise to the top, or whether such men will be held down by rigid caste or class restrictions.

He will want to know whether the people of a given nation are inclined to render blind obedience to those in authority or whether they tend to think and act for themselves. He will want to know whether the nation has developed a "code of honor" or a "code of a gentleman" which can be taken over and used by the officer group. He will want to know to what extent the average citizen is mechanically minded and trained. (If they are, it is much easier to form mechanized divisions.) He will want to know to what extent a martial tradition affects the bulk of the populace. These are only a few of the many problems which must be taken into consideration.

As a practical illustration of how social culture has influenced national character, it might be of interest to compare and contrast the people of India and China during a good portion of their historical development. Nearly all Hindus are intensely interested in religious beliefs and practices. Their religion may be a debasing superstition or an exalted philosophy, according to the nature and education of the person concerned, but one and all are interested in abstract speculation or devotional acts. On the other hand, they are little interested in concrete facts, especially historical facts. Although there is a vast literature written in Sanskrit and other Indian languages, the vast majority of the books composing this literature deal either directly or indirectly with religion. Works dealing with historical problems have been almost completely lacking until very recent times. As a result, for our knowledge of earlier Indian history we must rely upon ancient coins which have been unearthed in the last few decades, upon partially recovered inscriptions or half-destroyed monuments, and upon statements of occasional Greek, Arabic, or Chinese travelers who wandered in and out of India from time to time.

In contrast to this situation, most Chinese are not and

never have been interested in metaphysical speculation. The works of the so-called "Great Chinese Philosophers," such as Confucius and Mencius, ignore metaphysical problems and deal primarily with social ethics and with decorum. The problems which they seek to solve are: What is the proper relation between father and son? Husband and wife? Older brother and younger brother? The Chinese are enormously interested in historical facts, and until the Communists took over, they were first-rate historians. From the Chinese chronicles we can learn exactly what happened—to the year, the month, and even to the day—in the reign of Emperor Wu Ti in the second century B.C.

Material culture, in contrast to social culture, deals primarily with such problems as what people eat and drink. At first it may seem ridiculous to associate such problems with strategic intelligence, but this is far from being the case. In preparing war plans and counter war plans, it is essential to bear in mind the food habits of a given people.

In the event of war, we shall probably have to furnish our Turkish allies with huge quantities of food. In preparing shipments it must always be remembered that it would be tragic to send them canned ham because they would refuse to touch it. This ham, however, could and should be sent to our allies in Formosa, for the Formosans, like all other Chinese, relish pork in any and every form. I remember going to a banquet in Peking which consisted of thirty courses, and every one of these courses contained pork in some form or another. It should also be remembered that although there is no religious taboo on it, very few Chinese like the taste of beef. In the absence of pork, their favorite food is mutton.

The eating habits of the Japanese are very different from those of the Chinese. The basic diet of the Japanese consists of rice and fish. At one Japanese banquet I was served fifteen different types of fish, the favorite being *sashimi*, or raw fish. They also enjoy other food, such as eels and baby octopi. In the last few years many Japanese have learned to eat a little meat. However, they seldom like either pork or mutton, but are fond of beef.

The one food habit which the Chinese and Japanese have in common is a dislike of dairy products. Unless they have come under strong Western influence, neither the Chinese nor the Japanese will normally drink milk or eat butter or cheese.

If we ever have any allies in Hindu India (which I seriously doubt), we must never forget that there is a rigid taboo on the consumption of beef (or veal) in any form. The ordinary Hindu would rather starve to death than swallow a single piece of steak. As a matter of fact, many Hindus eat no meat at all, which is one reason why they tend to be less robust physically than the Pakistanis, who, being Mohammedans, are permitted to eat any meat except pork and do actually eat as much meat as they can afford. If we should have to supply our allies in Persia with food, it should be remembered that although they will eat beef, they are not very fond of it, their favorite food being mutton.

There are even notable food differences between the European peoples and between the Europeans and

Americans. Even British and American food likes differ to some extent. On many occasions during World War II, I had occasion to eat at the officers' mess attached to the Combined Chiefs of Staff, in which about half the officers were Americans, the other half British, except for a sprinkling of Dutch, French, and Poles. Very frequently, by observing what they were eating, I could recognize their nationality without glancing at their uniforms. This was especially true of breakfast. If I saw a man eating corn flakes and drinking coffee, I was certain that he was an American. If he were eating a bloater (a smelly fish) and drinking tea, I was sure that he was English.

There are also marked differences between peoples with respect to how food is eaten. Both the Japanese and the Chinese make use of chopsticks, which means that the food must be cut up into small pieces before it is cooked and served. In India and the Near East, except for persons who have been thoroughly Westernized, food is eaten with the fingers, or rather with the fingers of the right hand. One should never forget that it is very rude even to *pass* food with the left hand to any Arab.

In Europe and in America, everyone makes use of knife, fork, and spoon. There is, however, a marked difference between the American and the English use of these implements: the Americans are more acrobatic. When eating, say, roast beef and potatoes, an American will take his knife in his right hand and his fork in the left. But when he has cut up the meat, he lays the knife down, transfers the fork to the right hand, and proceeds to use the fork to shovel food into his mouth. Not so with the Englishman. He keeps his knife in his right hand and his fork in his left hand, even after the meat has been cut. He then uses his left hand to spear or harpoon his food and so get it to his mouth. It is astonishing how few exceptions there are to this general rule. One of the few exceptions that I have personally met is Dwight D. Eisenhower, who sometimes eats in the American and sometimes in the English manner.

Attention should also be paid to the drinking habits of a people. One should examine both what they drink and how they are affected by alcoholic beverages. There are alcoholics in all countries, of course, but I am inclined to think that there must be fewer in India than in any other country. In fact, the vast majority of the Hindus drink no alcohol at all. In contrast to this, I find that most Jews do drink, at least to the extent of taking wine, but I also find that very few Jews become confirmed alcoholics. I have no idea as to the reason for this. With many, though not all, of the Indians of North and South America, there is a tendency to go the other way. They tend to drink little or nothing, but when exposed to distilled liquors, they quite frequently drink to excess.

The Spaniards, the Italians, the Greeks, and the Armenians are acquainted, of course, with distilled liquor, but they are more apt to imbibe beer or wine. They may well drink three or four glasses of wine every day, but they seldom become drunk. If you see a man who is obviously under the influence of drink weaving down the streets of Naples, it is much more apt to be an American tourist than a native Neapolitan. The French also go in more for beer and wines than for spirits, but many of them drink enough wine to become drunk—or at least tipsy.

The drinking habits of the Turks and Arabs are very different from the group of peoples just mentioned. Being good Mohammedans, they should, of course, like good Methodists and Baptists, be total abstainers. But just as some Methodists and Baptists fall off the wagon, so do many Turks and Arabs, especially on a Thursday night (the equivalent of an American Saturday night). Possibly because of the fact that they make use of the maxim that you might just as well be hanged for stealing a sheep as a lamb, when they do drink, they are not satisfied with beer or wine but consume quantities of a distilled beverage called *Arak,* which is sometimes described as "hell on wheels."

The Chinese are acquainted with both fermented and distilled liquors. (One distilled beverage produced in and around Peking, called *Pai-ga-erh,* is, bar none, the worst-tasting drink in the world.) But although, on the average, the Chinese drink much more than do the Hindus, alcoholics are fairly rare. The chief weakness of the Chinese is not liquor but opium.

The drinking habits of the Japanese are rather peculiar. Normally they do not consume a great deal of hard liquor; but they are easily and quickly affected by what they do consume. They can become inebriated with a smaller quantity of alcohol than any other people I know. The same amount of drink which would put the average Japanese under the table would scarcely make the average Chinese merry. Again I do not know the reason for this fact. Possibly it has something to do with the small stature of the Japanese.

At one period I was able to make use of this weakness as an aid in securing military information. In 1937-38, I spent several months in and around Peking. This was at the time of the "China Incident," when the Japanese army was occupying a large part of North China. The American military attaché asked me if I would help him in securing information about the distribution of Japanese troops in the surrounding area.

Now most Japanese are fanatically loyal and patriotic, so I knew that it was useless to try to secure this information through bribing some of the officers or men. Instead, I began frequenting a Pekingese night club called the *Pai Kung*, or "White Palace," which was a popular rendezvous for Japanese officers when they came to Peking on furlough. I would sit patiently until one or other of the officers with whom I was acquainted came in. Inviting him over to my table, I would "treat" him to two or three Scotch and sodas. By the time he finished them, he would be a little "boozy" and I would begin to interrogate him. Even though he was tipsy, I knew that if I were to ask him where the regiment or division was, he would clam up immediately. Instead, I would casually ask him, "By the way Colonel, I have not seen you for some time. Where have you been keeping yourself?" By this time the influence of the alcohol would be such that my friend would not realize the importance of the question. He would say, "Oh, I have been in Hwailai." Now I already knew that the Colonel was attached to a certain military unit; hence it was easy for me to guess that his unit was in or near Hwailai. By following this technique with several other officers, in the course of a few weeks I had a fairly good picture of the Japanese order of battle in North China. But this experience left me with a permanent dislike of night clubs.

5

Ideological
Intelligence

THERE is another very important and much-neglected source of strategic intelligence. This is the careful study of the basic ideology (system of beliefs and value judgments) which is dominant in each country at any given time. It is especially important to study the basic ideology of the governing group in each country, whether or not this ideology is accepted by the bulk of the populace.

It is hard for the average American to accept the fact that ideologies are of importance in trying to estimate trends and tendencies. It is difficult for an American to understand that what a man believes can have any serious effect upon political or military actions. Certainly a man can be a good citizen and a good patriot, irrespective of the fact that he is a Jew, a Catholic, or a Protestant. Recent history, however, shows that military and political developments can be profoundly affected by the acceptance or rejection of certain ideas or doctrines, especially if these ideas or doctrines form part of a system which is designed to inspire its followers with fervent, fanatical zeal. In other words, through long experience, I am certain that ideas have consequences—and sometimes very important consequences.

During the 1930's, in connection with my university work, I had to make a careful study of the ideologies

87

which swept through Italy, Germany, and Japan, and I was able to make a number of predictions, most of which were subsequently verified. I could not, of course, foretell exactly when and under what circumstances World War II would break out, but I was certain that the Fascist-Nazi ideology would sooner or later lead to military aggression and hence to a major conflict. After the pact between Hitler and Stalin, I was sure that hostilities would break out within a very short time. It was easy for me to surmise that the Germans would make better soldiers than the Italians, if only because the Germans were more fanatical in their devotion to Nazism than the Italians were to Fascism.

The knowledge which I had picked up regarding certain phases of Japanese ideology were of considerable value to me in my work with the J.I.C. As a boy, living in Japan, I acquired a fairly intimate acquaintance with *Bushido*. *Bushido* was originally the code of the samurai, or warrior knights, but in modern times it became, in a slightly modified form, the code which all citizens, and especially all soldiers, were expected to obey. One phase of this code ruled "death rather than surrender"—in fact a man was told that he should commit suicide rather than fall into the hands of an enemy. I knew that most Japanese took this injunction very seriously.

In the spring of 1942, when I was permitted to look over the war plans which led to the invasion of Guadalcanal, I felt that not enough account had been taken of this aspect of the Japanese code of honor. The planners obviously took it for granted that when a Japanese garrison had been hopelessly defeated, were surrounded, and were starving, they would surrender. I insisted that very few Japanese soldiers would take this course. For some time my objections were brushed aside. But the actual events at Guadalcanal showed that I was right, and thereafter the plans were changed accordingly. In like manner, my study of *Bushido* enabled me to predict the coming of the kamikazes (suicide planes) several months before they began to operate.

In the spring of 1945, the Joint Strategic Survey Committee asked whether in my opinion the Japanese army would lay down its arms if ordered to do so by the Japanese government or would go on fighting to the bitter end. For a day or two I was hesitant about giving a definite answer. What I knew about *Bushido* did not seem to cover this situation. But eventually I wrote a paper stating that in all probability the Japanese army would meekly surrender *if*, but only if, the Emperor made a personal plea for this action. Secretly, I was not at all sure about the matter, but in the end, it turned out that I was correct.

Today it is clear that we must study a very different set of ideologies, but the fact remains that a careful study of the ideological systems which presently dominate large areas in Europe and Asia will give us a clue to probable political and military developments in the field of international relations. If time and space permitted, there are many different ideologies which are sufficiently popular to be worthy of serious consideration, but for the moment it is necessary to direct our attention to only three ideological systems because of their major importance. One of these ideologies I shall call (for want of a better term) "conservative liberalism." The second is Communism. The third is nationalism.

Conservative Liberalism

Conservative liberalism is the oldest and most widespread of the ideologies which are still important and influential at the present time. It is the ideological foundation upon which the American Declaration of Independence and the American Constitution are based, and it is still the prevailing ideology of the vast majority of the American people, whether they call themselves Republicans or Democrats. In a slightly different form it was preached by such great English thinkers as John Locke, Edmund Burke, and John Stuart Mill. It is still the most popular ideology both in Great Britain and in most of the nations comprising the British Commonwealth of Nations. But this ideology is not confined to the Anglo-Saxon peoples. It has spread to most of the countries of Western Europe, to nearly all of the countries of Latin America, and to many countries in Asia. Even Italy, Germany, and Japan, formerly dominated by Fascism and Nazism, are now governed by leaders and by parties dedicated to the principles laid down by conservative liberals.

Most students of history would be content to call this ideology by the simple name of "liberalism." In the last few years, however, especially in the United States, the word "liberalism" has come to be associated with various radical movements, even with Socialism and crypto-

Communism. For this reason it is necessary to use the term "conservative liberalism." Although it is possible to argue about the right name to be given this ideology, it seems clear that as a political creed, it is a compound of two separate elements. One of these elements is a belief in democracy; the other is a belief in individualism. Not infrequently these two elements are confused because of their long association with the liberal tradition, but it is well to keep the two doctrines clearly separate and distinct.

Democracy, of course, means the belief that ultimate political control should rest with the citizens of the country concerned, and more particularly with the numerical majority of such citizens, rather than be entrusted permanently to a single person or to any minority group. There are, of course, many types and degrees of democracy. In some countries democracy means that the right of voting and of being elected to office is open to all adults, whether male or female. In other cases women are ruled out and democracy means universal manhood suffrage. In still other cases the right to vote and hold office is limited by property or literacy tests. But even here the regime must be called democratic if ultimate control over the machinery of government rests with the bulk of the people rather than with a special minority. Under this definition, present-day England most certainly belongs to the group of democratic states, for although she retains an hereditary monarch and an hereditary House of Lords, all ultimate or final power rests with the popularly elected House of Commons.

Sharply distinguished from democracy is the doctrine

of individualism, which implies the right of each person to control his own actions as long as they do not seriously interfere with the liberty or the actions of others. Individualism asserts the right of each individual to "life, liberty, and the pursuit of happiness." Individualism is intimately associated with the concept of freedom: the freedom of each person to choose his own religion, absolute freedom of thought, freedom of speech and writing within the widest possible range, and the freedom of each person to choose, without government interference, the occupation or profession which appeals to him. Individualism implies belief in and respect for private property, the right of each person to control his own belongings as long as such control does not seriously interfere with the economic welfare of his fellow citizens.

Clearly, individualism is quite distinct from democracy, even though the two doctrines are not necessarily incompatible. It would be perfectly possible to have a regime which is completely democratic and yet which ignored the claims of individualism. Democracy, after all, is majority rule, and individualism asserts that even the majority has no right to complete domination of the action of majority groups or even over the actions of a single individual. In a country which is overwhelmingly Catholic, a popularly elected assembly might well pass a law forcing all citizens to join the Catholic church. Such a law would be thoroughly democratic, but it would be contrary to the tenets of individualism. In like manner, a country where the vast majority of the citizens were non-smokers might, through a popular referendum, pass a law prohibiting the use of tobacco by all persons.

Such a law would be democratic, but it would be in direct violation of the principle of individualism.

There are different types and degrees of individualism, just as there are different types and degrees of democracy. Some liberals have been convinced that individualism should be identified with strict *laissez faire*, that the government should in no way interfere with the economic life of its citizens. Other liberals, including the majority of conservative liberals, insist that true individualism permits a certain amount of governmental regulation of commercial and industrial life on the ground that under a system of *laissez faire* the private individual may fall victim to some of the great monopolistic enterprises and hence cease to have real freedom of action. It should, however, be stressed that conservative liberals, unlike some radical groups which call themselves liberal, have a firm belief in the value of free enterprise as the general basis of economic life. They admit that some government regulation and control may be necessary but that it should be severely limited in scope. They assert that the motto should be: "As much regulation as necessary, but as little as possible."

In the present work we are not concerned with attacking or defending the position assumed by the conservative liberals. Our main interest is in foretelling how certain countries will act. For this reason we need only state that in the immediate future those countries which are governed by persons or parties which are favorable to conservative liberalism will tend to be friendly to the United States and will seek to align themselves with America by means of diplomatic and military pacts. In the period immediately following World War II, among the prominent representatives of conservative liberalism were Churchill in England, Adenauer in Germany, de Gasperi in Italy, Yoshida in Japan, and Magsaysay in the Philippines. All of them were strongly in favor of maintaining close and friendly ties with the United States. Many of these men have now disappeared from the political scene, some through death, some through retirement from active life. But they have left successors. Generally, it may be said that the Conservative party in England, the Liberal-Democratic party in Japan, and the Christian Democratic parties of Germany and Italy represent different phases of the conservative-liberal movement and that as long as these parties remain in power in their respective countries, these countries will remain pro-American in their basic attitudes.

Right-Wing and Left-Wing Totalitarianism

The direct opposite of conservative liberalism is totalitarianism. If conservative liberalism may be called a combination of democracy and individualism, totalitarianism is a combination of authoritarianism and collectivism or statism. The principle of authoritarianism is the antithesis of the principle of democracy. There have been and still are many different versions of the authoritarian creed, just as there are many different forms of democracy, but all forms of authoritarianism agree in rejecting majority rule and substituting for it a strong government centered in either a single person, a comparatively small group of persons, or at the most a single party.

If authoritarianism is the opposite of democracy, so is statism the direct opposite of individualism. Because of their emphasis upon the state and their rejection of individualism, the statists believe that the state not only may but should curb the actions, the speech, and even the thoughts of its citizens when any action, speech, or thought is contrary to the aims which the state sets for itself. To the statist, not only should the state abolish all pretense of freedom of speech, freedom of the press, and the right of free association, but it should also set rigid limits to religious toleration, lest devotion to the doctrines of the Church interfere with devotion to the dictates of the state. Even the spread of philosophical and scientific ideas must be watched closely and, if necessary, stopped if these ideas appear inconsistent with the ideas which have been established by the state.

The thoroughgoing statists go even further and insist that the state must exercise a rigid censorship over literary, artistic, and musical movements on the ground that widespread acceptance of certain literary, artistic, or musical ideals might injure the morale of the populace and thus indirectly injure the power and prestige of the state. It goes without saying that the statists are vociferous in their claim that the state must exercise strict and complete supervision and control over the economic activities of its citizens. Many go further and insist that the state should own and operate the means of production and distribution. The more thoroughgoing statists believe that not only commerce and industry but also agriculture should be collectivized and nationalized.

Logically, it would appear that there is no necessary connection between authoritarianism and statism. It would be perfectly possible to have an authoritarian state (i.e., one controlled by a small aristocracy or by a single person) which allows the private citizen a great deal of individual freedom. Such, in point of fact, was Russia under the old Czarist regime. In like manner, it is perfectly possible to have a strict statist regime which is controlled by the bulk of the people and thus form a democracy. Such, in fact, is the type of state dreamed of by many socialists in both ancient and modern times. It so happens, however, that just as conservative liberalism grew up as a combination of democracy and individualism, so has the totalitarian tradition grown up as a combination of authoritarianism and statism.

As we have already seen, there are several different types of totalitarianism. At the moment, however, it is necessary to indicate only two main types because it is these two and only these two which have played a major role in the shaping of modern history. One of these we may call right-wing totalitarianism, as exemplified by the Fascist-Nazi ideology, to which the governments of Italy, Germany, and Japan were fanatical adherents for a number of years. The other type we may call left-wing totalitarianism, and it is represented by Marxist or Communist ideology, which completely dominates and motivates the governments of the U.S.S.R. and China today— to say nothing of the puppet governments set up by the Communists in a number of satellite states. To some persons the placing of Fascism-Nazism and Communism in the same general category may seem astonishing because of the bitter hostility which sometimes existed between the Fascist-Nazi regimes, on the one hand, and the

Communist regimes, on the other. But a careful study of the two ideologies shows that they are very closely related, both in theory and in practice.

The principal difference between the Fascist-Nazis (or Nazi-Fascists) and the Communists is that the latter are more careful to hide, or rather to camouflage, their ultimate aims and purposes. The Nazi-Fascists were frank in their dislike of democratic institutions and openly admitted that they wished to establish an authoritarian, or dictatorial, regime. The Communists claim to be devoted to the principles of democracy, even of extreme democracy, but close examination shows that their claim is completely fraudulent. Even Marx was forced to admit that to him, democracy meant not majority rule but "the dictatorship of the proletariat"—even when the proletariat constituted only a small section of the total population. In point of fact, when the Communists come into power, it is not even a "dictatorship of the proletariat." In Communist-controlled states, absolute power is placed in the hands of a single party (the Communist party), but only a fraction of the total number of citizens are allowed to join this party and share in its privileges. In turn, the party is completely controlled by a small number of high-ranking officials, very few of whom have come from the working classes. In most cases ultimate power tends to gravitate into the hands of a single dictator.

In like manner, the Nazi-Fascists frankly admitted that they disliked and despised the whole principle of individualism and were wholehearted in their admiration of statism. The Communists, on the other hand, claim to be devoted to individualism. They assert that it is only through Communism that man achieves freedom or liberty. They proclaim that under Communist leadership the state will eventually "wither away," leaving mankind in a sort of Utopian anarchy. Actually, however, the Communists are just as ruthless and relentless in their emphasis upon statism as were the Nazi-Fascists. Under a Communist regime the state retains a rigid and minute control over all forms of economic activity. All of the basic instruments and organs of production and distribution are directly owned and operated by the state. But this strict statism is not confined to the economic area. Under Communist regimes a citizen is compelled to accept the dictates of the state in every phase of his personal and private life. If a man writes a novel, composes a symphony, or paints a picture which is not in accord with the cultural standards laid down by the state, he must expect swift punishment at the hands of the secret police. No one is free to propose or defend any philosophical or scientific theory which is not in accord with the dogmas laid down by the state. Even the thoughts of the citizens are curbed by means of "brainwashing."

Communism

In the 1930's and 1940's, it was necessary to study both the Nazi-Fascist and the Communist forms of totalitarian ideology. However, the utter destruction of the Nazi-Fascist regimes as the result of World War II means that for the moment we can omit any serious examination of right-wing totalitarianism in our study of international relations. A careful consideration of left-wing totalitarianism, or Communism, on the other hand, is more necessary than ever because of the enormous increase in the size and strength of the Communist countries in the last few years. The entire question of the peace of the whole world, of victory or defeat, even of the survival or extinction of the whole world, depends in large measure upon an understanding of the capabilities and intentions of the Communist regimes.

For those interested in the subject, it is not difficult to arrive at an adequate comprehension of the basic tenets of the Communist ideology. All of these tenets have been clearly laid down in the writings of the major Communist leaders. Of special importance are three basic books. One of them is *Das Kapital,* by Karl Marx, one is a book by V. I. Lenin called *State and Revolution,* and one is a book by Joseph Stalin called *Problems of Leninism.* The personal downgrading of Stalin in recent years does not alter the fact that Stalin's work is still of importance in trying to understand the development of Communist ideology.

It is not necessary to stress the importance of an adequate understanding of the ideas expounded by Marx. To be sure, the life and writings of Marx belong to the nineteenth and not to the twentieth century. The *Communist Manifesto* was written in 1848, more than a hundred years ago. His first (and most important) volume, *Das Kapital,* was published in 1867, and Marx himself died in 1883, but we must never forget that the ideology formulated by Marx is still the dominant ideology of the whole Communist world. All Communists, even today, unite in regarding Marx as the inspired prophet of the "New Dispensation" and his writings as the authoritative exposition of eternal truth. It is for this reason that a perusal of *Das Kapital* is of especial importance. But it must be remembered that the work consists of three hefty volumes and that the style is far from easy.

In this brief study it is impossible to deal with the abstract and purely theoretical aspects of Marxist philosophy. We have neither the time nor the space to deal with the dogmas regarding dialectical materialism, the labor theory of value, and the theory of surplus value. It may be remarked that all of these dogmas are completely rejected by everyone except the devoted followers of Marx, but a detailed consideration of such matters lies outside the scope of our present undertaking. As students of political realities, we are, for the moment, more concerned with the practical conclusions which Marx drew from these three dogmas.

It is important to remember that Marx thought of himself not as a social philosopher but as a social scientist. He was convinced that his new system, based on the dogmas mentioned above, not only gave him a scientifically accurate analysis of the social and economic conditions of his own times but also provided him and his followers with a method by means of which they could predict, with almost mathematical certainty, future developments in the economic, political, and military spheres. *Das Kapital* is not at all a plea that men ought to accept Communism; it is essentially an elaborate analysis showing that certain developments will necessarily and inevitably take place, irrespective of whether the bulk of mankind does or does not approve of them. It has been estimated that in the course of his writings Marx made more than 150 definite predictions regarding future developments. It has also been estimated that more than 90 per cent of these predictions have turned out to be completely erroneous.

We cannot deal with these predictions in detail, but it may be of interest and value to point out one particular group of forecasts. Not only did Marx insist that the triumph of Communism throughout the world was inevitable, but he also insisted that he knew when and how and where the Communist revolution would break out. According to the Marxist system of analysis, the Communist revolution would necessarily start in the highly industrialized and highly capitalized areas of the world—the bigger and better the industrialization, the bigger and better the growth of capitalism, the sooner the inevitable revolution. Following out this line of argument, Marx made the definite prediction that the outbreak of the revolution would take place in such areas as England, Germany, France, or possibly the United States of America. He made the further prediction that the revolution would not and could not take place in such backward areas as Russia and China.

It is interesting to note that when the Communist revolution did take place, it broke out exactly where he told us that it could not take place and did not break out where he told us that it had to take place. Incidentally, Marx's basic assumption that the growth of capitalism and the growth of the Communist movement necessarily go hand in hand has proved fallacious time and again. Even in Asia the revolution did not break out in Japan, the most highly industrialized of all Asiatic nations, but in relatively backward China. And in China itself the development of the Communist movement did not take place in the big industrialized cities of Tientsin, Shanghai, and Canton, but in the relatively backward areas of North and Northwest China.

Although all of Marx's basic assumptions are fallacious and although the vast majority of the predictions he made on the basis of these assumptions have proved definitely false, we must not blind ourselves to the fact that Marx has won an enormous number of converts, most of whom are animated by a fiery and fanatical devotion to the Marxist creed. For this reason it is absolutely essential that we constantly bear in mind one or two other features of the Marxist ideology. One of these is the doctrine that the Communist revolution cannot be a partial or a limited revolution but must be world wide in scope. Marx vigorously rejected the idea that the Communist movement could be confined to a single country or to a single continent. He rejected the idea that it was possible for the world to be divided among several different powers, each with its own ideology. He insisted that his followers should seek to overthrow each and every one of the governments which refused to accept the "dictatorship of the proletariat." He insisted that his followers constantly aim at the domination of the whole world.

We must never forget that the true Marxist refuses to believe in the possibility of an enduring peace between

Communist and non-Communist nations. The true Marxist believes that there is and must necessarily be perpetual war between the Communist and non-Communist forces. Sometimes this war may be a hot war, sometimes it may be a cold war, sometimes it may be a lukewarm war, depending upon the strategic position of the Communist forces at the moment. But in one form or another, the war must go on until the non-Communist forces have been completely vanquished. The true Marxist is prepared to negotiate a truce between campaigns, but to his mind, the truce is merely a convenient interval permitting the Communists to re-form and rebuild their depleted forces and prepare for a new and more vigorous attack, either in the same place, or else in some other, more favorable area. The true Marxist categorically denies the possibility of long-term "peaceful co-existence."

Another basic feature of the Marxist ideology which has been accepted by all the later Communists is that in their struggle to secure and maintain power, the Communists must be bloody, ruthless, and relentless. They despise any and every form of toleration and humanitarianism. Any tendency to avoid shedding blood, any notion that it is wrong to kick a man when he is down and that it is noble to spare a defeated foe, were regarded by Marx as weak and decadent. The Marxist thinks of his enemy as the enemy of mankind, and that is why he calls the extermination of his opponents, not murder, but "the liquidation of unsocial elements." His ruthlessness in dealing with his opponents is the direct result of the logic of his doctrine. In his opinion, he is only doing what dialectical materialism decrees that he must do.

Associated with this doctrine is the complete and absolute rejection of traditional or conventional morality. According to Marx, the Ten Commandments are arbitrary inventions of the greedy exploiters of the proletariat and hence could and should be ignored by the true Communist. To lie, to steal, to cheat, to deceive, to murder is not bad, but good, if such action promotes the sacred cause of Communism. According to Marx, the true Communist must be prepared to make wild promises, with no idea of carrying them out; to make wild and reckless charges, if such charges weaken the opposition (hence the completely baseless charge that the Americans were carrying on germ warfare in Korea). The true Communist must be prepared to make and to tear up any solemn treaties at will, to make non-aggression pacts, so as to throw non-Communist nations off their guard, and then make sudden, bold, and vicious attacks on these nations when a favorable opportunity arises. To a Marxist, there is no such thing as good or bad; there are only some things which do and others which do not promote the success of the Communist cause.

On most points, the later Communist leaders have been content to follow blindly in the footsteps of Marx, but on two or three vital points, Lenin and his successors have made significant changes in the Marxist program. For the most part, these changes did not necessitate any serious modification of the basic ideology as laid down by Marx, but they did necessitate a marked modification of ideas with regard to the best strategy to be used in securing the success of the Communist movement. It was Lenin who was primarily responsible for the decision to make use of the rural and agrarian populace in the struggle to place the Communist party in power. Marx himself was concerned only with the urban and industrial element in the population. Marx disliked and despised the peasant, the tenant farmer, the sharecropper, and the landless agricultural laborer. Such persons played no part in his program for active revolution. He believed that they were inclined to accept the ideology of the *bourgeoisie* and hence would tend to be enemies of the Communist cause.

Lenin, however, was shrewd enough to realize that the agrarian populace could be used as valuable allies or, rather, as easily manipulated tools by the Communists in their struggle for power. At the time of the Russian Revolution, the Russian Communist party consisted of a small and insignificant group of persons. The people who might be regarded as their natural allies, the Russian factory workers, were few in number and too weak in influence to place control over Russia in the hands of Lenin and his followers. Lenin therefore made a bold move: he declared that the Communists were the natural protectors of the agrarian populace. He promised, moreover, that if he were placed in power, the big estates would be broken up and that the land would be distributed, without cost, among the peasants and agricultural laborers.

Lenin's appeal to the agrarian populace met with immense success. The Russian peasant knew nothing and cared nothing about Marx and Marxism. He never bothered his head about dialectical materialism and the surplus theory of value, but he was enormously attracted by the promise of free land, and it was primarily because of peasant support that Lenin was able to secure power. It goes without saying that as soon as the Communists had consolidated their position they lost interest in the peasants and in the peasant ownership of land. The big landowners did, indeed, lose their estates, and for a very brief period the "little fellows" were allowed to take possession of the land, but before long the Communist program called for the collectivization and nationalization of all arable fields. Those peasants who tried to cling to their newly won possessions were ruthlessly liquidated.

What is especially interesting in this connection is the fact that the Communists, inspired by their success in Russia, continue to make use of the same technique in other countries—and with a considerable amount of success. There can be no doubt that much of the support which the Chinese Communists secured during their early struggles with the Chinese Nationalists came from the poorer section of the agrarian populace, who were inspired by the Communist attacks on "the selfish and greedy landlords" and by the promise of the redistribution of land. Following Russia's example, the Chinese Communists climbed to power largely through the support of the peasants.

Again following Russia's example, the Chinese Communists, having consolidated their power, have already begun to take away from the peasants their newly won land in the name of collectivization and nationalization. We have already witnessed a brutal and ruthless liquidation of a large section of the Chinese farmers, but this

does not prevent the Communists from making successful use of the same facile promises in other lands. Much
of the support which the Huks had in the Philippines
and which the Indian Communists have had in India
came not from factory workers but from disgruntled
peasants who were and have been lured into the Communist camp by promises of "land reform."

In point of fact, to an impartial and scientific observer,
there is serious doubt as to the amount of economic good
to be accomplished by the wholesale redistribution of
land, even when there is a genuine and well-meaning
attempt to do so. In some cases it brings about economic
benefits, as evidenced by an increase in the total amount
of crops harvested, but in other cases it brings about
economic harm, as evidenced by a decrease in the total
amount of crops harvested, resulting in less food available for the general population.

In pre-Revolutionary Russia there was much to be said
for some sort of land reform. There were many thousand-
acre, ten-thousand-acre, and even hundred-thousand-
acre estates, and many of these huge estates were waste-
fully and inefficiently managed. The break-up of these
estates and the development of peasant proprietorship
would probably have aided Russia's economy. In China,
on the other hand, there was a very different situation.
Really big estates, in the Russian sense of the term, were
almost unknown. A three-hundred-acre estate was considered enormous, and from such statistics as are available, it would appear that the average prosperous land-
lord owned about fifty or sixty acres. In nearly all cases,
these fifty-acre estates were broken up into fractional

holdings—plots of an acre, or half an acre, or even a fourth of an acre. Such fractional holdings have proved to be economically unsound. The real truth of the matter is that in China, as in many other Asiatic countries, there are just too many people and not enough land, with the result that *no* scheme of land distribution can bring about economic prosperity.

As long as we are concerned with a study of Communist intentions, we are not called upon to face or to solve this problem. What we can assert, however, is that Communist agitators will continue to make use of the same or similar techniques in order to stir up trouble in other parts of the world. Wherever there is a severe population pressure resulting in widespread poverty among the rural and agrarian population, we can expect to find Communist agents at work, proclaiming that if the populace will only support the Communist cause, everyone will secure an adequate amount of free land and poverty will thereby be abolished. Conditions in Java, in India, and in many of the countries of the Near East, especially Egypt, present an enticing field to Communist agitators who have been trained to use slogans of "agrarian reform" in their efforts to bring about a collapse of the existing regimes.

Another major modification in the original Marxist strategic program was the emphasis upon nationalism and upon the support of nationalist agitations as a means of spreading Communist control. This modification was also initiated by Lenin but has been developed and perfected by his successors. It must be remembered that Marx himself was not in the least interested in the cause

of nationalism—in fact he placed himself in violent opposition to all national movements. He regarded nationalism not as an ally but as a deadly rival to Communism.
He was horrified at the idea that the Italians, or the Russians, or the Chinese, or the inhabitants of India, should
get together and form a united front, irrespective of class
differences. To his mind, the dominant slogan was
"Workers of the world, unite," without regard to nationality.

Marx was not only opposed to nationalism, but in
addition, he was a serious advocate of the principles of
imperialism and colonialism, on the ground that the
building up of vast colonial empires was a useful and
even a necessary step in the development of world Communism. He wanted to have world power concentrated
more and more into the hands of a few great nations. The
more powerful these great empires became, the greater
and more rapid would be the development of industrial-
ism and capitalism within their borders. This, in turn,
would lead to the more rapid development of the Communist movement and to the outbreak of the great
Communist revolution. Once the mother country was
controlled by the Communist hierarchy, the colonies and
the dependencies would automatically fall into the Communist orbit.

Marx's basic thought ran somewhat as follows: It is
useless to try to Communize India directly because India
is too backward industrially to be receptive to Communist propaganda, but if England controls India and
the Communists seize power in England (which is ripe
for the Communist revolution), then the Communists

would seize control of India. In like manner, why try to Communize such a backward country as Russia? Why not let Germany conquer the whole of Russia? The Communization of Germany would then automatically bring Russia within the Communist fold.

Lenin, being a very capable and shrewd person, realized that Marx had made a fundamental mistake in his strategy. Like Marx, he had no real use for the principle of nationalism, but he saw that the various nationalist movements (especially the nationalist movements in Asia) could be made into useful tools in the spread of Communist control. He realized the enormous force and driving power that lay behind these nationalist movements, and instead of trying to suppress them, he determined that these movements were to be encouraged in order to bring about the overthrow of existing governments. At the same time, careful, elaborate, and successful efforts were made to see that the leadership of these nationalist movements was infiltrated by trusted Communist agents so that such movements could be made to follow the dictates of the Kremlin.

It goes without saying that the support which Lenin and his successors gave to the nationalist movements of Asia is based upon deception and fraud. Smal-Stocki's book on *The Nationality Problem of the Soviet Union* shows how brutally the Kremlin authorities treat any genuine nationalist movement once they have complete control over an area. Nevertheless, it is clear that the Communist hierarchy has in several instances met with signal success in using nationalist movements as weapons with which to strike blows at the Western powers in general and at America in particular.

As the result of subtle but effective Communist propaganda, many of the illiterate masses of Asia have come to believe that the U.S.S.R. is the genuine friend of the upsurging nationalist movements and that the United States is the spearhead of reactionary European imperialism. We know that the Chinese Communists have utilized this idea to strengthen their position in China and in Korea. We can see an interesting and dangerous example of this situation in Indochina. The North Vietnam forces of Indochina are entirely controlled by Ho Chi Minh, who is a wholehearted Communist, and yet by posing as the advocate and protector of Indochinese nationalism, he has been able to win warm support from millions of people who have no use for Communism whatsoever. In the near future, we must be prepared to see the Kremlin attempt to use a similar technique in other parts of Asia and in Africa as well.

So far we have dealt primarily with Marx and with Lenin and his successors, the leading representatives of European Communism. It is now necessary to say a word about Mao Tse-tung and the other representatives of Chinese Communism. During the crucial years from 1945 to 1950, there were a great many persons in America who came to realize the true nature of European Communism but who continued to insist that Chinese Communism represented something very different. The vast majority of writers during this period insisted that the Chinese Communists were not really Communists at all—they were agrarian reformers, they were forward-looking liberals, they were anti-Fascist progressives, they were this, that, and the other thing, but, it was said, they were certainly *not* Communists. This whole notion was (and is) complete nonsense.

Since I became personally involved in this conflict, I feel that I must go a little more into detail. Having spent so much of my youth in the Far East, I have always retained an interest in the social, economic, and political developments in this area, even when living elsewhere. In the 1920's, I read a great many accounts of the formation and development of the Chinese Communist party, but in the absence of first-hand information, I kept an open mind on the subject. During the period from 1937 to 1938, I was again in China and came into close contact with many Communists and Communist sympathizers. At this time I was *almost*—but not quite—sure that the Chinese Communists were radical Marxists and would act accordingly, but not being sure, I refused to dogmatize.

From 1942 to 1944, when I was working with the J.I.C., I was somewhat puzzled by several secret dispatches sent back from China by some of our young foreign-service officers stationed there. According to these dispatches, the so-called Communists were really not Communists at all but earnest and idealistic reformers. I said to myself that I had been wrong in my judgment. I was glad, therefore, when, in the spring of 1945, I was sent on a special mission to China and had a chance to talk with some of the leading representatives of the principal political groups, including the Communists. In addition, I read a great many of the articles and pamphlets put out by the Communist press.

I soon came to the conclusion that our young foreign-service officers had been hopelessly misled. I found that the Chinese Communists made no attempt to hide their true ideology, which was orthodox Communism—not Socialism or Communism in general, but the Marxist form of Communism as modified by Lenin. I was certain that if the Communists conquered China, she would certainly turn her back on the free world and would rapidly drift into the Russian orbit. When I returned to America, I made a report to my superiors to this effect. I soon found that my report was in substantial agreement with a report prepared by a group of Army officers in the Pentagon.

Under pressure from the State Department, our views were rejected, and when General Pat Hurley, our Ambassador to China, came back and made a similar report before a Congressional committee, he was forced to resign his ambassadorial post.

I returned to civilian life at the end of 1945, but in 1947, I was appointed consultant to the Congressional Committee on Foreign Affairs and was again sent on a special mission to the Far East and spent some time in both Korea and China. In 1948, on my return, I made both verbal and written reports to the Committee. It was in this report that I specifically predicted that Communist North Korea would invade South Korea if we withdrew all of our divisions from the latter country. I also predicted that if we gave aid to Nationalist China, the Communists could be suppressed but that if this aid was not given, the Communists would conquer all of China within two or three years. I predicted that this would be disastrous to American interests. It would mean the end of our cherished Open Door Policy of "special privilege for none; equal opportunity for all." I was certain that under the Communists, equal opportunity for American citizens would be a thing of the past. I was also certain that the Communists would so harass our citizens, whether businessmen or missionaries, that they would be forced to flee and that all American property would be confiscated.

About the time that I made my report, General Wedemeyer made a similar report to the Secretary of State. It was all to no avail. General Wedemeyer's report was suppressed, and my report was ignored. At the same time that we were telling the French and Italians that they would get no American aid unless they kicked the Communists *out* of the government, we told the Chinese that they would get no aid unless they took the Communists *into* their government.

After the Korean Communists invaded South Korea, and more especially after the Chinese Communists came to the aid of the North Koreans and openly fought against American troops, the majority of Americans came to their senses and realized the true nature of Chinese Communism. However, there is still a substantial minority who refuse to believe that the Chinese Communists are not wholehearted Marxists and that if the United States would only appease them, they would be lured away from their Communist inclinations.

Nationalism

It now becomes our task to attempt to summarize the ideology of nationalism—especially that extreme form of nationalism which prevails in many Asiatic countries —and then see how this ideology is likely to affect international relations.

At the start it must be confessed that it is much easier to make an estimate of Communist intentions than nationalist intentions because control over all Communists is highly centralized, while there is no such centralization among the various nationalist groups. All true Communists—whether American, French, Italian, or Indian —want and intend exactly what Moscow orders them to want and intend. Among the various nationalist groups, on the other hand, there is no such unity of purpose and command. What the fiery nationalists of India want is obviously not what the equally fiery nationalists of Pakistan want and intend—and so on with the other countries dominated by ultra-nationalist ideologies.

Nevertheless, a careful study of the various nationalist movements, in particular a detailed study of the ultra-nationalist movements now dominant in many parts of Asia, does bring to light a remarkable similarity in ideological pattern. By studying this pattern, we should be able to gain some insight into probable trends and intentions among the leading exponents of extreme nationalism.

In the first place, attention should be called to the intensity and fanaticism of Asiatic nationalism, a fact

115

which many Americans have failed to take into consideration. Speaking in general terms, we may say that the Asiatic nationalist is four or five times as fanatical as the ordinary European nationalist. We tend to think of the Irish and the Poles as being extremely nationalist. For the most part, they are, but the intensity of their feeling pales into insignificance when compared to that of the typical Asiatic nationalist.

There is one basic reason for the difference in intensity between the European and Asiatic nationalists. Nationalism in Asia is especially fiery because it is a very new movement thrust upon peoples with very old civilizations. For some curious reason, nationalism in action is like a childhood disease: the later in life you get it, the more severe a case you have. As everyone knows, if a child of six or seven gets an attack of measles, or mumps, or whooping cough, it is usually not a matter of great importance. The mother, naturally, worries a great deal, but for the most part, the child is well again in a short time and, moreover, is immune to a recurrence of the same disease. With an adult, on the other hand, things are far different. If the father of the child contracts the same disease for the first time, things are apt to be more serious and there is need to look out for complications. It is still worse—far worse—if it is not the father but the grandfather who catches the disease. Such a case usually calls for a nurse twenty-four hours a day. So it is with nationalism. Those countries which are converted to nationalism fairly early generally get a rather mild reaction, those which go nationalistic later on generally have a heavier dose, and the last to adopt nationalism as a basic ideology are apt to have a terrible case.

Most of us are apt to forget that what we now call nationalism is a concept which has developed only in comparatively recent times. A brief glance at history will remind us that in ancient Greece, for example, there was very little of what we would now call nationalism. At that time there was a great deal of fighting and a great deal of patriotic feeling, but the fighting was between, and the patriotism was centered around, the various city-states, such as Athens, Thebes, and Sparta. The Greeks were very proud of being Greeks and thought of all non-Greeks as barbarians. But it never seems to have occurred that the Greeks constituted a "nation" and should have been unified into a nation-state.

In like manner, there was very little of what we call nationalism in ancient Rome. Almost overnight Rome jumped from a city-state to a world empire and never passed through the stage of being a nation-state. Hence in the whole of Roman history there was almost never anything corresponding to what could be called Roman or Italian nationalism. Likewise, in the Middle Ages we can find only a trace of nationalism. During this period fighting of some sort was going on constantly and more or less universally, but it was based on such things as feudal rights, or women, or religion, and almost never was the principle of nationalism involved.

We do, indeed, find a trace of nationalism at the time of the Reformation with the development of Lutheranism in Germany, Anglicanism in England, and Galli-

canism in France—but nowhere did this incipient nationalism burst into full flower. Even in the seventeenth
and eighteenth centuries nationalism played an insignificant role in international affairs. Most of the wars waged
during this period were dynastic wars and were concerned with whether this or that territory was to be governed by the Bourbons, the Hapsburgs, or the Hohen-
zollerns, and no one stopped to ask to what "nation"
the territory in question rightfully belonged. In the
eighteenth century we witness the rise of the important
new ideology centered around the "natural and inalien-
able rights of man," but it is to be noticed that people
were talking about the rights of man in the abstract, not
about the particular rights of Englishmen, Frenchmen,
Germans, or Italians.

The real rise of nationalism as an important factor in
international relations took place about 1800, during the
latter part of the French Revolution. The first major
spokesman for nationalism as a basic ideology was the
German philosopher J. G. Fichte, who was active during
the first decade of the nineteenth century. The first concrete expression of the nationalist principle in the practical sphere of politics, war, and diplomacy was centered
around the Greek War of Independence during the
period from 1815 to 1830. After the success of the Greek
nationalist movement, the whole idea of nationality and
nationalism spread like wildfire all over Europe. Within
a few years we witness the rise of fiery nationalist movements in a number of different countries.

It is noteworthy, however, that those countries which
had already achieved their unity and independence prior

to 1830 developed only a mild form of nationalism. We may say that the nationalism which developed in such countries was a sound and healthy form of nationalism; witness, for example, the nationalism of England, France, and the United States. On the other hand, those countries which did not secure their unity and independence until the middle or the latter part of the nineteenth century developed a more intense form of nationalism; witness the cases of Germany and Italy. In like manner, those countries which secured their unity and independence only during the early part of the twentieth century developed an especially fiery type of nationalistic ideology; witness the cases of Ireland and Poland.

Turning now to Asia, we find that Asiatic nationalism as a real factor in international affairs was practically non-existent until 1900. We can be more specific and date the rise of nationalism in Asia as a major factor in world affairs from the winter of 1904-1905. This was the period of the Russo-Japanese War, and the success of the Japanese in their conflict with Russia had a great deal to do with the fomenting of nationalism in all parts of Asia. The Russo-Japanese War led to the revolt of Asia against "white supremacy," and the leaders of this revolt found it convenient to adopt and then further develop the nationalist ideology, which was already current in Western Europe. In developing this ideology, the Asiatic leaders changed nationalism from a political to a religious creed. In trying to estimate what an Asiatic country is likely to do, or intends to do, we must never forget that in all probability the country in question will not follow a logical or rational pattern in the course of its action if such a pattern conflicts with some of the dogmas derived from its nationalist ideology.

There is another very curious feature about nationalism which applies to both Europe and Asia. For some reason or other, most nationalist movements begin as literary movements, then become political movements, and end up as military movements. Go back to the origin of most nationalist movements and you will usually find a little group of long-haired men and short-haired women who get together to smoke cigarettes and to talk about poetry, folklore, and folk dances. This group is interested in studying and popularizing ancient legends and traditions; not infrequently, it is interested in reviving an ancient language which is threatened with extinction. At first there is not a word or a thought of politics, but soon someone suggests that something practical should be accomplished, that the state should be forced to take a hand in the revival of the national language and the national traditions. Before long the literary movement is transformed into a political movement. If the political movement has difficulty in accomplishing its purpose, before many years have elapsed some bright and eager young man, carried away by the strength of his convictions, reaches under his bed one night, gets out a gun, goes out, and starts shooting. He is joined by a few enthusiastic comrades—and now we have a full-fledged military movement.

A very curious and important feature of nationalism is the fact that so many of the nationalist movements—both in Europe and in Asia—have been led either by foreigners, semi-foreigners, or else by what we may call "deracinated persons." First of all, let us deal with the case of foreigners and semi-foreigners. In studying the history of the rise of nationalism, it is amazing to see how many nationalist movements were led by men who had no real connection with the nationality in question. The most important figure in the Greek nationalist movement was not a Greek but an Englishman, or rather a Scotsman, with the very un-Greek name of Charles Gordon Byron. Lord Byron was, of course, primarily a poet, but he eventually became interested in politics. Because of a personal scandal he had to leave England. After a brief stay in Italy he went over to Greece to be an active leader in the Greek revolution and "to die that Greece might live."

I am especially interested in the history of the Greek nationalist movement for personal reasons. One of my collateral ancestors was one of the minor leaders in this movement. The man in question was an English country doctor named John Scott. He did not speak a word of Greek and had not the remotest connection with Greece, but he became enormously excited about the cause of Greek independence. He gave up his practice in England and went to Greece to serve in Lord Byron's army. As a soldier, in spite of his enthusiasm, he did not have a very successful career. A few months after his arrival in Greece he was captured by the Turks. The Turks were just about to shoot him when he managed to persuade them that they might find his medical service of value.

Dr. Scott's life was spared, and while he was a prisoner of war, his services as a doctor came to be more and more esteemed by the Turkish army. In the end, he was called to serve as physician in the harem of the Turkish Sultan. All of this sounds very interesting, but if Dr. Scott told the truth in his diary, this period of his life turned out to be very dull. He was never allowed to see any of his female patients. The ladies of the harem would thrust an arm through a curtain so that he could feel their pulse, but this was the only portion of their anatomy that he could feel or even look at. He was thus under a very severe handicap in trying to make a diagnosis. But Dr. Scott was either very lucky or else very shrewd because he was credited with several remarkable cures. In the end he was freed and sent back to England, laden with gifts. Subsequently, he came to the United States, and his descendants are now scattered over America.

I have referred to this little episode in my family history merely to show that people can get mixed up in nationalist movements with which they have absolutely no personal connection. History reveals hundreds of other examples. Historians have always been interested in the career of Charles Stewart Parnell, one of the outstanding leaders of the Irish nationalist movement during the middle and latter parts of the nineteenth century. Parnell was a very great man, worthy of esteem, but it remains a fact that this leader of Irish nationalism can scarcely be called a true Irishman. Though Parnell was born in Ireland, his father was of pure English stock, and his mother was an American. As far as is known, there was not a drop of Irish blood in Parnell's veins. Moreover, he was very untypical of Ireland and the Irish. We tend to think of Irishman as being fluent talkers, as liking a little alcoholic refreshment, and as staunch Catholics. In contrast to this, we find that Parnell was a rather poor speaker, was practically a "teetotaler," and was a staunch Protestant—but these facts did not prevent him from becoming an outstanding champion of the Irish cause.

Another interesting example comes from Germany. One of the most powerful of ultra-nationalists in Germany, the man who can be regarded as Hitler's spiritual father, was Houston Stewart Chamberlain. Chamberlain was a pure-blooded Englishman; in fact he was a distant cousin of Neville Chamberlain, one-time Prime Minister of England. Although born and brought up in England, Houston Chamberlain went to Germany as a young man and fell in love with the country and the people. He married a German girl (the daughter of Richard Wagner, the noted composer), became a German subject, and proceeded to write a number of books in German. The most important and influential of his works was his *Grundlage des Neunzehnten Jahrhunderts* (*Foundations of the Nineteenth Century*), a monumental two-volume work published in 1900. Of very great importance is the fact that the ideas embodied in this book became the foundations of the whole Nazi ideology. In fact, we may say that Hitler's *Mein Kampf* is only an extended footnote or a sequel to Chamberlain's major work.

So far we have dealt only with Europe. Let us now turn to Asia. By this time we should not be surprised to find that the real founder of the Indian nationalist movement was not an Indian at all but an Englishman named Allan Octavian Hume. Hume, a charming and delightful member of the (British) Indian Civil Service, thought the Hindus spent too much time in abstract speculation and were not taking sufficient interest in social, economic, and political issues. It was for this reason that in 1885 he was instrumental in founding the Indian National Congress. At first he experienced great difficulty in getting any considerable number of Hindus to join, and it was not until the twentieth century that the Congress began to attract widespread attention and support.

If the leaders of nationalist movements are not foreigners, in many cases they are semi-foreigners. The classical example of such a case is Adolf Hitler. Hitler was undoubtedly the greatest—or at least the most influential—of all the German nationalists, and yet, technically, he was not a German at all but an Austrian. To be sure, the Germans and the Austrians have many things in common, but there *is* a difference, and it will be remembered that Hitler had considerable difficulty in legally becoming a German citizen so that he could hold office in the German Republic. Perhaps the very fact that he had to struggle to become a German made him more fiery and fanatical in his devotion to German nationalism than were many persons who were German by birth.

Another interesting example of a semi-foreigner as a nationalist leader is the case of Eamon de Valera, for many years the Prime Minister of Ireland. There can be no doubt of the ability and sincerity of de Valera, but it is somewhat amazing to find that this fiery leader of Irish nationalism had a Spaniard for a father and that he himself was born in Brooklyn, New York. His only connection with Ireland was through his mother.

We should also bear in mind the case of Rudyard Kipling, the great English poet and short-story writer. Not only was Kipling a leader of English nationalism, but he has also told us how he came to be linked with this cause. Kipling had an English father and mother, but he himself was born and reared in India. In spite of the fact that so much of his life was spent abroad, we find in Kipling a much stronger devotion to England and all things English than is characteristic of the bulk of the people born and brought up in London, Manchester, or Liverpool. Kipling wrote a poem on the subject, one line of which reads: "What do they know of England, who only England know?" What he is really trying to say in the whole poem is that "I, who lived so much abroad, realize the glory and majesty of England much more than any person who has spent all his life in England can be expected to do."

Thus far we have dealt with those leaders of nationalist movements who were either foreigners or semi-foreigners. It is now time to discuss the case of those persons whom we have called "deracinated persons." In some respects such persons are the most important of all, certainly as regards Asiatic and African nationalism. It is from a study of such people that we can gain our best insight into certain trends which are especially characteristic of nationalist movements in Asia and Africa, and from these trends we can build up an estimate of the probable intentions of the major Asiatic and African nations.

The term "deracinated person" is somewhat peculiar and requires a little explanation. A deracinated person is a man (or a woman) whose roots have been dug up from his (or her) native soil and then transplanted in alien soil. Better than a definition is to cite such outstanding examples as Gandhi and Nehru in India and Sun Yat-sen in China. We might also cite Sukarno, the outstanding leader of Indonesia, Jinna, the creator of Pakistan, and Nkrumah, the leader of Ghana in Africa.

To get a clearer understanding of what is meant by the term, let us make a brief examination of a typical deracinated person. Because he is the best known to the American public, let us start with the case of Gandhi. Gandhi had, of course, an Indian father and an Indian mother, and he was born in India, but when he was in his teens, he was sent to England, not merely to receive an English education, but to be made into an English gentleman. In those days he did his best to act, to feel, and to think as an Englishman. At this time he did not insist on wearing only a loincloth; he was quite content to dress like a typical upper middle-class Englishman. He learned how to play the violin and how to dance in the European fashion. In those days he knew little and cared less about the cultural heritage of India. Though he remained nominally a Hindu, he knew almost nothing about Hinduism. He had never even read such sacred books of Hinduism as the Vedas and the Upanishads. His first acquaintance with Hindu thought came through perusal of Sir Edwin Arnold's *Song Celestial,* a beautiful but not very accurate translation of the *Bhagavat Gita.* Gandhi succeeded in his ambition and become a good Englishman. Then came the tragedy. The British sneered at him and continued to refer to him as a "native." They refused to accept him as an equal or even as an Englishman.

Quite understandably, as time went on, Gandhi became more and more embittered, and in the end he became violently anti-British. The movement he led and the political philosophy he formulated played a major role in driving the British out of India. But what is of major interest and significance is the fact that Gandhi's political philosophy, about which there is so much talk, borrowed very little from traditional Hindu ideology. Traditional Hindu ideology was completely oblivious of the very idea of nationalism and of national self-determination. Traditional Hindu ideology, being intimately associated with caste, was violently opposed to all notions of equality and democracy. Gandhi's two pet slogans were *Swaraj* and *Swadesh* ("self-rule" and "self-support"), yet both of those terms were completely unknown in India before the beginning of the twentieth century. So alien was Gandhi to traditional Hindu ideology that it was small wonder that he met his death at the hands of an orthodox Hindu.

If one takes the time to read Gandhi's autobiography, where he frankly traces the genesis of his ideas, it will be found that nine-tenths of his ideology is really derived from Western sources. There were three Western authors from whom he derived especial inspiration. One of them was John Ruskin, one of the founders of British Socialism; another was Leo Tolstoy, the noted Russian novelist; and the third was Henry David Thoreau, the New England exponent of naturalism. It was from Ruskin that Gandhi got his dislike of capitalism; it was from Tolstoy that he got his doctrine of pacifism; it was from Thoreau that he got his doctrine of passive resistance. (In this connection, it should be emphasized that the foregoing statements are in no way an attack on Gandhi's philosophy. They are merely an attempt to show that this philosophy was not indigenous to India but was imported from abroad.)

In many ways the career of Nehru closely parallels that of Gandhi. Like Gandhi, Nehru is a typical deracinated person. He, too, was born in India of Hindu parents and was sent at an early age to be made into an English gentleman. Coming from a wealthier and more aristocratic family than Gandhi, Nehru went to Harrow, a fashionable English boarding school, and then to Cambridge, a fashionable English university. He did well at both places, with the result that he speaks and writes perfect English, and many persons claim that he understands England and the English better than he understands India and the Hindus. He is frank to admit that he is unsympathetic toward conventional Hindu ideas and ideals and that his own beliefs are almost entirely derived from English and other Western sources. At the same time, we must not forget that Nehru was bitterly anti-British and that he still views the British with dislike and suspicion. Of even greater importance, to us at least, is the fact that Nehru was (and still is) definitely unsympathetic toward Americans.

Nehru is not a Communist and at times has treated Indian Communists with some severity; but he is inclined to be sympathetic to the Russians, largely because the Russians have usually been anti-British and anti-American. His antagonism toward the United States is so great that it is ridiculous for us to think that we can make him pro-American overnight by granting India large sums of money. I do not believe that Nehru wishes to see the United States completely destroyed, but he would thoroughly enjoy the spectacle of our losing a great deal of prestige. If I may be permitted to use a rather vulgar phrase, I would say that he would be delighted to see us soundly kicked in the rear end—especially if some Asiatic people, such as the Chinese, were to do the kicking.

Turning from India to China, let us draw a thumbnail sketch of the man whom the Chinese know as Sun Wen and whom we know as Sun Yat-sen. Dr. Sun is another outstanding example of a deracinated person. He was born in China (near Canton) of Chinese parents, but most of his early years were spent in Hawaii, then an American territory, and in Hong Kong, a British colony. His education was almost entirely Western. Years ago, when I was a young man and Dr. Sun was already an old man, I had an opportunity to have several talks with this distinguished statesman, and I still remember how amazed I was to find how little he knew about ancient Chinese culture and ideology. To him, such ancient sages as Confucius, Mencius, and Lao-tse were little more than names, but he was thoroughly familiar with such men as Abraham Lincoln, Thomas Jefferson, Tom Paine, Henry David Thoreau, John Ruskin, and G. B. Shaw.

When I met Dr. Sun, I had just read his most noted book—the book which has become the Bible of Nationalist China. This book, *San Min Chu I* (*Three Principles of Government*), attempts to deal with the three basic principles of government, which are listed as (1) Nationalism; (2) Democracy; and (3) *Min Sheng,* usually translated as "Welfare Statism." I remember asking Dr. Sun, "Where did you get the idea of the three principles? I have read my Confucius and my Mencius and I know that neither of these sages had anything to say about such things as Nationalism, Democracy, or the Welfare State." Dr. Sun laughed, patted me on the back, and said, "My boy, it should have been obvious to you, an American, that I got these three principles from Lincoln's Gettysburg Address, with its phrases 'government of the people, by the people, for the people.' Government of the people means Nationalism; Government by the people means Democracy; and Government for the people implies the Welfare State."

But the fact that Sun Yat-sen derived most of his ideas from the West did not prevent him from being bitterly anti-Western in general and anti-American in particular.

Did space permit, I should like to go into the biographical and cultural background of the other important leaders of Asiatic and African nationalism, but being pressed for space, I can only say that with rare exceptions all of these leaders follow a similar pattern. They are nearly all men who were educated in the West, adopted Western culture and ideology, and then became bitterly antagonistic toward Westerners.

It is necessary to draw attention to one further characteristic of most nationalist movements, a characteristic which is likely to cause some difficulty in the years ahead. Most nationalist movements, as they develop and become successful, tend to become imperialistic. This statement may seem strange to some persons, for we tend to think of nationalism as the direct opposite of imperialism. However, a careful study of history shows that for the most part, nationalism is baby imperialism and that imperialism is grown-up nationalism. This holds true for both Europe and Asia.

In the middle of the nineteenth century, the Italian nationalists were concerned only with achieving *Italia liberata,* an Italy free from all foreign control, but only a few years later, when unity and independence had been secured, the force of Italian nationalism led to the conquest of Libya, Ethiopia, and Albania. In like manner, during the middle of the nineteenth century, German nationalists asserted that their only goal was a free and united Germany. This goal was duly achieved, but only a few decades later the German nationalists were talking about *Lebensraum* and thus were led to demand control over Czechoslovakia, Hungary, and the Ukraine.

In view of this situation, it is not surprising that many of the leaders of Asiatic nationalism have shown marked imperialistic tendencies. Sun Yat-sen, the founder of Chinese nationalism, spent most of his time preaching against imperialism, but he insisted that China retain control over Mongolia, Chinese Turkestan, and Tibet— in all of which areas the Chinese constitute a very small minority. In fact, he insisted that the boundaries of the Chinese Republic should be the same as those of the ancient T'ang Empire, which would mean that China would control more than half of Asia.

The Indian nationalists are also showing several signs of incipient imperialism. As long as non-Hindus were ruling over Hindus, the Indian nationalists were all in favor of self-determination, but once the British were forced out of India, these same nationalists changed some of their attitudes. In this connection it is interesting to remember what happened in Hyderabad and Kashmir. Hyderabad was a large and important state in Central India which enjoyed almost complete autonomy, even during the period of British domination. It was controlled by a native monarch, the so-called Nizam. All of the cabinet ministers were also natives of Hyderabad. But it so happened that the Nizam and most of the high officials were Mohammedans, while about 85 per cent of the general populace were Hindus. The Nizam wished Hyderabad to remain an independent nation when the British withdrew from India, but, using the preponderance of Hindus as an excuse, Nehru ordered the Indian army to move in, and Hyderabad was forcibly annexed to India.

Shortly afterwards, the case of Kashmir arose. Kashmir was another large, semi-autonomous state. It was ruled over by a Maharaja who happened to be a Hindu, though more than 85 per cent of the inhabitants were ardent Mohammedans. The Maharaja declared that Kashmir should form a part of India, though it was clear that the overwhelming majority of the Kashmiris opposed this move, since they wished to join Pakistan. On the ground that the Maharaja's wishes should be the determining factor, Nehru immediately sent Indian troops to occupy the area. Since that time he has consistently refused to permit a plebescite to be held, for the very good reason that he knows that such a plebescite would go overwhelmingly against him. Hyderabad and Kashmir together constitute a classic example of the old rule, "Heads I win, tails you lose."

Many of the Indian nationalists have even wider territorial ambitions. They have openly declared that they will never be satisfied until the whole of Pakistan is incorporated within the boundaries of India, irrespective of how the Pakistanis feel about the matter. They also announce that they intend to seize control over Goa, or Portugese India, although a free and fair plebescite of the inhabitants of this area showed that well over three-fourths of them wished to retain their ties with Portugal.

Two other examples of nationalism changing into imperialism are to be found in Indonesia and in Egypt. Sukarno, the dictator of Indonesia, is not content with driving the Dutch out of his country; he now demands control over Western New Guinea, although the inhabitants of this area differ profoundly from the Indonesians as regards race, language, and culture and show absolutely no desire to be incorporated into Indonesia. In like manner, Nasser, the dictator of Egypt, is not content with the fact that the British have completely withdrawn from Egypt and that the Egyptians are absolutely free of foreign rule. He wishes to see Egypt made into a huge empire embracing all states with an Arabic-speaking population, irrespective of whether the inhabitants of these other Arab states do or do not wish to be drawn under Egyptian control.

II
THE SHAPE OF
TOMORROW

6
Prospects
for the Future

In the preceding chapters I have endeavored to show how different methods and techniques can be used in the preparation of intelligence estimates. We are now faced with an even more difficult problem: Is it possible to combine these various methods and techniques in such a way as to prepare general or overall estimates of what is likely to take place in the immediate or foreseeable future? I think it can be done.

In this connection it may be well to define more clearly and simply what is meant by strategic-intelligence estimates. Such an estimate must give a list of our actual and potential enemies and then seek to analyze their probable intentions and capabilities. We must also attempt to assess the intentions and capabilities of those nations which are now neutral but which may become inimical or friendly in the near future. Finally, it is necessary to make a list of our actual or potential allies and analyze their probable intentions and capabilities in order to secure a better view on our own defensive and offensive positions at any given time.

Such an estimate must cover not only the periods when actual fighting is taking place (the periods of so-called "hot war") but also the long periods of "cold war" when no serious fighting takes place—when the various nations jockey for position and when they continue to engage in diplomatic, economic, and psychological warfare.

The Communist Nations

When we draw up a list of our most serious and dangerous enemies, it is essential that we place the Communist countries at the head of it. The most deadly enemies are, of course, Russia and China, but the various satellite nations must also be included because they will be forced to carry out all orders issued to them by their Russian and Chinese overlords.

There are still many persons in the United States who think that it is possible to stop the cold war and to ease the tensions between the Communist world and those nations which are still free. I am deeply convinced that such persons are completely wrong. I thoroughly agree with the statement made by Dr. Bertram D. Wolfe (*New Leader*, January 26, 1959):

The Soviet system of power . . . is a deadly enemy. It is a deadly enemy because never for a moment does it abandon its two basic aims: to remake men and to conquer the world. It is particularly our enemy—not because we so choose, but because it has chosen. It regards the strength and the way of life in the United States as the chief obstacle in its plan to remake its own people and to remake the world in the image of its blueprint. We have been picked as Enemy Number One.

No matter what the President says or does, no matter whether the Secretary of State conducts himself with tact or tactlessness, we would still be Enemy Number One. Whether our working class is prosperous, or hungry and jobless, or jobless and not hungry, we will still be Enemy Number One. Whether we pull out of Berlin and Quemoy or do not pull out of Berlin and Quemoy, we can not disengage ourselves from this enemy.

Let us not listen to the siren song of those who tell us that we can get a release of "tensions" and a little peace in our time if we only "disengage" ourselves. If we disengage ourselves, we leave another strip to be occupied, a new place from which battle will begin.

It should be emphasized that when Dr. Wolfe speaks of the "Soviet system of power," he means both the Russian *and* the Chinese governments. There are some who believe that whereas Communist Russia may be our "Enemy Number One," Communist China is of minor importance. This is completely erroneous. Communist China is even more implacable in her hatred of the United States. She is equally determined that the Communist system shall dominate the whole world and that the continued strength of the United States is the principal obstacle to the world-wide triumph of Communism.

The Russians are convinced that it is only the United States which prevents them from overrunning the whole of Western Europe. The Chinese are equally convinced that it is only the United States which prevents them from engulfing all those portions of the Far East which are still free. It is the common hatred of the United States which is the strong bond holding the Russian and Chinese empires together.

In some ways Communist China is somewhat more of a menace to American interests than Communist Russia.

The Russians, much as they hate the Americans, are well aware of the real strength of the American armed forces and will be hesitant about provoking an all-out shooting war in the immediate future. Because of the relative success of the Chinese army in Korea (at a time when the Americans refused to employ nuclear weapons or even to make use of conventional bombing beyond the Yalu River), the Chinese have somewhat less respect for the military might of the United States. There are many of the younger leaders in Communist China who tend to think of the United States as a "paper dragon," fearsome in outward appearance but weak and powerless in reality. For this reason they are more willing to face the United States in a head-on collision. It is the Russians who retain greater caution, who will act as a brake against any attempt by China to provoke World War III before overall Communist strategy is ready for it.

There are many who believe that by diplomatic negotiations it would be possible to drive a wedge between Russia and China. There are some who think that it is possible to make a "deal" with Russia at the expense of China. There are many more who think that it would be possible to make a "deal" with China at the expense of Russia. I am deeply convinced that all such ideas are completely illusory. It is quite possible, to be sure, that after a lapse of five or six decades changes in the hierarchical structure of either Russia or China, or a serious alteration in the balance of power between the two nations, may bring about a sharp cleavage between the two major Communist states (if the Communist system lasts that long). It is even conceivable that a century from now the United States and Russia may be linked in an alliance to check Chinese aggression. But for the present and for the foreseeable future, strategic estimates must be made on the assumption that Russia and China will remain closely linked together. It is not that the Russian and Chinese *peoples* feel any great love for one another. It is, rather, that Russia and China are both ruled by a small number of fanatical Communists who feel that it is only through a close liaison between the two countries that they can bring about the Communization of the world.

Although the Communist powers are determined to avoid all-out peace (by giving up the cold war), I am convinced that for the near future, at least, they are equally determined to avoid an all-out war. I am certain that if, when, and as the Communist powers feel that they have far surpassed the United States in nuclear weapons and ICBM's and that if, when, and as the Communist powers believe that they are in a position to destroy the United States without undergoing shattering damage themselves, they will launch a surprise attack on Europe and America, using all the weapons at their disposal. But that time has not yet come.

Both the United States and Russia have nuclear weapons, but there is good reason to believe that the Russian A and H bombs are no better than our own, that Americans still have a larger stockpile of these bombs, and that we can continue to out-produce the Russians. At the moment it would appear that the Russians are slightly ahead of us in the production of intercontinental ballistic missiles on which to mount nuclear

141

bombs, but the gap between the Russians and the Americans is rapidly narrowing and should soon be closed. In the meantime, we have a better strategic air force, both as regards quantity and quality. The Russians will have to send their bombers into the air from bases behind the Iron Curtain, while we still have strategic air bases in Europe, North Africa, and Asia capable of launching massive attacks at a moment's notice. We are still far ahead of the Russians with respect to nuclear weapons launched from submarines, and we still have a monopoly of atomic submarines.

Our armed forces must always be ready to resist and to retaliate in the event of a surprise attack. But as long as our men are thus kept in readiness, the outbreak of an all-out shooting war, though possible, is not probable. This, in turn, means that neither the Russians nor the Chinese are likely to carry out such actions as would inevitably lead to such an all-out war. This brings us to a discussion of the Berlin problem in the West and the Formosa problem in the East.

The Russians are desperately anxious to secure control of West Berlin for many reasons. There is serious unrest, not only in the satellite nations, but also in the Soviet Union itself. A successful attempt to secure West Berlin would give the Russians so much added prestige that some of this dissatisfaction would be quieted. (A victory abroad always softens domestic unrest.) Again, Russia feels humiliated by the constant flow of refugees from East Germany into West Berlin and would like to plug this hole. Finally, the economic progress made in West Berlin, in contrast to the stagnation in East Berlin, is very bad for Communist public relations.

As a result, the Russians will do everything, *short of war*, to try to induce the Western Allies to get out of West Berlin, thus leaving this area to the tender mercies of the East German puppet government. They will try to persuade and cajole. They will use every kind of threat and bluff. They will make every effort to bring about disunity among the Western Allies, leading to a weakening of the Allied position in Berlin. But if the Allies remain firm and united, if they clearly indicate that they will remain in West Berlin, using force if necessary, I am convinced that the Russians will back down. The Russian army could easily overrun Berlin if it chooses, but if the Russians believe that such a step would lead to all-out war, they will, in all probability, refrain from taking that step.

In like manner, the Chinese Communists are desperately anxious to secure control of Formosa and the coastal islands (Quemoy and Matsu). Unrest in China is even greater than in Russia. There are frequent outbreaks of resistance to Communist tyranny in many of the rural areas. The Chinese Communist leaders believe that much of this unrest and revolt would be quieted if they could secure control of Formosa and the lesser islands. These leaders also believe that if they can induce America to withdraw support from this area they will have gained a tremendous psychological victory. The prestige of the United States would be so lowered all through those portions of the Far East which still remain free that the absorption of the whole of the Far East into the Communist empire could be effected with no great difficulty.

For this reason I am convinced that the Chinese Communists will continue to make every effort, *short of war,* to secure Formosa and the other islands. They will bring constant pressure upon American public opinion to permit them to occupy, first of all, the coastal islands, knowing that if they succeed in doing so, Formosa itself will collapse. If they fail in this effort, they will try to persuade the Americans to neutralize Formosa itself or permit it to be placed under a United Nations trusteeship. This would end the independence of Free China, a step which would be almost as favorable to Communist aims as the actual occupation of Formosa by the Chinese Communist army.

However, if the United States, in the face of blandishments and threats, remains firm and lets it be known in an unmistakable way that if the Communists undertake a military campaign to secure the Formosa–coastal islands area they will be met with immediate counterattack by American forces, it is very unlikely that such an attack will take place. From a strictly military point of view, it would be as easy for the Chinese Communists to occupy the coastal islands as it would be for the Russians to occupy Berlin, but if the Chinese Communists knew that such a step would lead to all-out war, in all probability they would refrain from such an attempt. Sporadic bombardment of the islands may well continue, but a serious effort to land forces on them, though possible, is not very likely.

If I am right, the Russians and the Chinese, for the immediate future at least, will refrain from such actions as would lead immediately to an all-out global war. But it is certain that they will continue to engage in an active and widespread cold war. It is highly probable that this cold war will entail some actual shooting, through small-scale, limited, local wars, in which we must be prepared to participate.

In this connection, I should like to point out that the American Joint Chiefs of Staff were guilty of a serious mistake in drawing up their estimates of enemy intentions from 1945 to 1950. During this period the Chiefs and their advisers were firmly of the opinion that we were faced with either all-out war or all-out peace. They believed that the era of local or limited wars was over, that if the Communists were to attack at all, they would start with a major land offensive in Western Europe or with an air attack upon the United States—or possibly both.

For this reason the Joint Chiefs were completely surprised when the Communists started their offensive in Korea. As a consequence, for several weeks we were ill prepared to counter this attack. If tentative war plans had included the possibility of a campaign in Korea, we could have had more and better-trained combat troops available and could have moved them with greater speed and effectiveness. In the absence of a sufficient number of tactical bombers and men trained to use them, we had to make very inadequate use of strategic bombers.

The lessons learned in Korea had to be learned all over again when, a short time later, the Communists attacked in Indochina. Because of inadequate planning, we were not in a position to assist the anti-Communist forces at Dien Bien Phu and Northern Vietnam was taken over by Communist forces. Happily, some of the earlier errors have been rectified, so that in 1958 we were able to land an adequate number of troops in Lebanon after only a few days' warning.

It is impossible to predict exactly when or where the Communists will launch the series of "brush fire" wars which are to be expected in the next few years. Although rigid as regards their ultimate goal, the Communists are very flexible as regards the tactics employed to achieve this goal. Being opportunists, they will strike at any time or place that the local conditions appear auspicious. This might be in Latin America or in Africa south of the Sahara. But for many reasons, especially economic reasons, trouble is more likely to arise in the Near East and in Southeast Asia. We must keep our eyes on both of these areas, and at the same time, since the Communists would like to throw us off balance by striking first at one and then at the other.

I am convinced that the Russians will make repeated efforts to secure control over the whole of the Near East because if they did so, they would be able to wreck a large part of NATO's war effort. This is because of the petroleum situation. It is fairly certain that although Russia would like to secure Near Eastern oil for herself, she has no crying need for it, but she has, and will continue to have, a strong desire to deny this oil to our allies in Western Europe. To the NATO nations, Near Eastern oil is of crucial importance—so important that victory or defeat may well depend upon it.

It is estimated that if World War III were to break out in the near future, the oil wells in the United States and other parts of the Western Hemisphere would produce all the petroleum needed for the American army, navy, and air force. But it would not be enough for us *and* our European allies. To provide for the oil requirements of England, France, Germany, and the other NATO nations, it would be absolutely necessary to have access to the Near Eastern oil fields. This means that if Russia can secure control of the Near East, she will have conquered the West without striking a direct blow at any European nation. The guns, the trucks, the tanks, the ships, and the airplanes of Western Europe would be immobilized, while the Russian forces would be free to move around at will.

In this connection a distinction must be made between the centers of oil distribution and those of oil production. Neither Egypt nor Syria has any oil fields of importance, but nearly all of the oil produced farther to the east has to pass through these two countries. In normal times, about 50 per cent is carried in tankers which pass through the Suez Canal. The other 50 per cent is sent through a series of pipelines, most of which cross Syria in order to reach the Mediterranean. As long as Syria and Egypt were two separate countries, it was possible to use one source of supply if the other was blocked. Now that the two countries have been joined to form the United Arab Republic, it means that a single man, such as Colonel Nasser, can, at a moment's notice, stop the flow of oil to the West. It is small wonder, therefore, that Russia is making and will continue to make every effort to bring the United Arab Republic into its orbit.

But that is not enough because it does not involve the oil-producing areas, which are in Iraq, Kuwait, Saudi Arabia, and Iran (Persia). With time and effort, the

West could provide other methods of transporting this oil to Europe. It could complete one or more pipelines through Turkey. It could build larger tankers capable of carrying huge quantities of oil around the Cape of Good Hope. This, in turn, means that Russia will earnestly seek to seize control of all these oil-producing areas. It is possible that Russia will permit Colonel Nasser to unite all of the Arabic-speaking areas (Iraq, Kuwait, and Saudi Arabia) with his United Arab Republic. It is more likely, however, that the Russians will endeavor to install separate governments in each of these areas, governments even more subservient to the Communists than the United Arab Republic.

In order to accomplish their purpose, the Russians will continue to use psychological, diplomatic, and economic warfare, but if necessary, they will use armed force. I doubt that they will send in large numbers of Russian troops, but they will make use of Arab stooges to create riots and rebellion aimed at overthrowing any government which remains friendly to the West. The bloody revolution in Iraq in 1958 is probably only a sample of what is to come.

Turning now from the Near East to Southeast Asia, I am convinced that the Chinese Communists will make every effort, including the use of armed force, to secure control of all the countries in this area. This means that Communist China intends to gain control of the whole area once known as Indochina. She already has control over North Vietnam. She is determined to browbeat South Vietnam into submission, and, by a mixture of subversion and military intervention, she intends to secure control of the little kingdoms of Laos and Cambodia. Next it will be the turn of Thailand (Siam) to be "liberated." This should prove a fairly easy task unless the United States intervenes. After that, the Communists will move west and take over Burma. I do not believe that the Chinese intend to invade India in the near future. Instead, after securing Burma, they will turn southeast and engulf Malaya and Singapore, for them a very valuable area. After a brief pause, they will seek complete domination of Indonesia—the old Dutch East Indies. Ultimately, the Chinese would like to secure control of the Philippine Islands, but because of the American position there, there is little likelihood that they will make any serious move in this direction in the immediate future.

There are many reasons why Communist China should turn her attention to Southeast Asia, but perhaps the most important single factor derives from the economic situation. Russia wants to control the Near East, not so much for her own economic advantage, but to deprive the West of much-needed oil. China, on the other hand, wants Southeast Asia, not so much to deprive the West of vitally needed strategic raw materials, but to bolster her own economy.

China is now in much the same position as was Japan before World War II. The Communist rulers of China are determined to make her a major power, both from the military and from the industrial point of view. China, in spite of her huge size and enormous population, is woefully lacking in many of the essential raw materials needed to accomplish this purpose. She has plenty of coal but very little iron ore. She has adequate supplies of tungsten but very little of the more important ferro-alloys, such as chrome and manganese. At present, China, with her own resources, can produce only about ten million tons of steel a year. Mao Tse-tung and his cohorts want to increase this amount fivefold, but in order to do so, they must have control over the iron ore and the ferro-alloys to be found in Southeast Asia. They will not be content to have commercial access to this area, but will insist on complete military and political control.

In like manner, China is very weak, even weaker than Japan, as regards the domestic production of petroleum, but the oil wells of Burma, Sumatra, and Borneo would give her an ample supply of this vital raw material. China has an urgent need of the nickel to be found in Celebes. If she is to embark on large-scale airplane production, she has great need of the bauxite deposits to be found in several of the Indonesian islands.

Earlier in this book I made reference to the intelligence estimate, made early in 1942, of Japan's probable war plans, based on her need for raw materials. I am convinced that at the present time this old estimate could be dusted off and, with slight verbal changes, be labeled "The Probable War Plans of Communist China." In other words, just as Southeast Asia was vital for the war aims of Japan during World War II, so is this same area vital for the war aims of Communist China at the present time.

Neutralist Groups and Nations

A study must be made of certain neutralist groups and nations because a slight shift in their attitudes might have an important effect on the world situation.

Socialist Groups

Attention should be given to the Socialist parties in various parts of the world, with special attention to those Socialist parties which constitute a leading minority in their own countries and which, at any election held in the near future, may become the majority party and thus be placed in charge of the government. Such, for example, are the Socialist parties in England, Germany, Italy, and Japan.

It is no part of our undertaking to discuss the merits or disadvantages of Socialism as an economic or political creed. We are concerned only with the foreign policy of these various Socialist groups and the attitude they take or are likely to take in the cold war between the free world and the Communist powers.

It is, of course, necessary to bear in mind that there is a marked difference between the ordinary Socialists and the Communists (though the latter frequently refer to themselves as Socialists). The Socialists are nearly all devoted to democratic principles, while the Communists go in for a rigid dictatorship. For this very reason, while the Communist parties all over the world carry out the plans prepared in the Kremlin, the Socialist party of each

STRATEGIC INTELLIGENCE AND THE SHAPE OF TOMORROW

nation formulates its own programs and policies. Moreover, even within the Socialist party of any one state, a wide variety of ideas and aspirations is tolerated.

Among most Socialist parties, however, there is a strong tendency to form a more moderate, or "right wing," group and a more radical, or "left wing," group. In Italy there are, indeed, two separate parties, a right-wing Socialist party led by Saragat and a left-wing Socialist party led by Nenni. In England, in Germany, in Japan, and in most other countries, both groups are contained within a single party, but there are sharp differences of opinion between the two groups.

For our purposes it is important to bear in mind that most right-wing Socialists are fairly firm in their opposition to Communism and the Communist nations, while most left-wing Socialists tend to think that it is possible to come to a long-term understanding with the Communists through appeasement or "disengagement."

To put matters more concretely, in England, if the Conservatives lose power and are succeeded by a Labor government, there is bound to be a change in British foreign policy. As long as Gaitskell, a right-wing Socialist, remains leader of the Labor party, England will not break completely with the Western Alliance, but there will probably be a demand that the United States give up her atomic air bases in Great Britain, and there will certainly be a weakening of the British stand against Russia. It can also be confidently predicted that England would increase her demands that Communist China be admitted to the United Nations and be given a seat on the Security Council.

In Germany, a Socialist victory would also have important consequences in the field of foreign relations. There are many Socialists, such as Mayor Brandt of West Berlin, who are firm in their opposition to Communist aggression, but if Ollenhauer, the leader of the German Socialist party and himself a left-winger, were to become Chancellor, there is a strong chance that Germany would shift to a neutralist position.

In Japan, the situation is even more dangerous. The right-wing Socialists are already neutralists and wish to abandon Japan's treaty with the United States. The left-wing Socialists, who control most of the party machinery, go even further. They would welcome an understanding or even an alliance with Communist China and Russia. If a general election were to result in the formation of a Socialist government, it would be necessary for the United States to make a radical change in its strategic planning, and hopes of using military bases in Japan as a guard against renewed aggression by Communist China would have to be abandoned.

Indonesia, India, the Arab Nations, and Black Africa

We must also turn our attention to those countries in Asia and Africa in which the governments are in the hands of extreme nationalists. Are such countries likely to side with the Communist powers or with the free powers in the event of an armed conflict between the two groups? How are such countries likely to behave during a long-term continuance of the cold war?

153

In the past, most Americans have tended to believe that Asiatic and African nationalists would automatically side with the free world in the struggle with Communist aggression. For many years past, imperialism and colonialism have been unpopular with the American public. As a result, the Americans have generally sympathized with the Asiatic and African peoples in their revolt against European domination. The United States gave the Philippines complete independence in 1946. She ended her occupation and control of Japan and Korea at the earliest possible moment. She played a major role in forcing the Dutch to grant independence to Indonesia. She warmly welcomed Britain's withdrawal of political control over India, Ceylon, and Burma. Most Americans rejoiced at the complete withdrawal of France from Indochina, once it seemed reasonably certain that this action would not result in a Communist take-over in that area.

In like manner, American public opinion rejoiced when Lebanon, Jordan, and Syria became independent states. In the struggle between the British and the Egyptians, the Americans have tended to sympathize with the Egyptians. Most Americans rejoiced when the British Gold Coast colony in West Africa became the free state of Ghana. They look forward to the time when Nigeria and other Negro colonies become independent nations. In the struggle which is going on in South Africa between the blacks and the whites, most Americans have tended to sympathize with the blacks.

Because most Americans are friendly to the Asiatic and African nationalists, they tend to take it for granted that these nationalists are and will continue to be friendly to the United States. Unfortunately, in a great many instances, this is far from being true. The revolt of Asia and Africa against Europe tends to be identified in those areas with the revolt of various dark-hued peoples against white supremacy. Since the Americans are predominantly white, this means that most Asiatic and African nationalists look upon Americans with deep and dark suspicion. They tend to think that any interest which the United States shows in Asia or Africa is based upon a subtle plot to secure American political domination over the whole of Asia and Africa and to subject the inhabitants of these areas to ruthless capitalist exploitation.

This conception is, of course, completely without foundation, but this fact does not prevent it from being accepted by many millions of Asiatics and Africans. The mere fact that the United States has been willing to grant to many Asiatic and African peoples huge sums of money, either as loans or else as outright gifts, has not improved the situation. It is impossible to buy friendship or love; in addition, many Asiatics and Africans look upon this financial aid as a subtle imperialist plot.

Fortunately, not all of the countries governed by extreme nationalists share in this erroneous concept. Generally speaking, those countries which lie in close proximity to the Communist powers have come to realize the real danger to themselves of Russian and Chinese aggression and as a result have become friendly to the United States and the other free nations. Thus the nationalists of South Korea, South Vietnam, Thailand, Pakistan, Iran, and Turkey have become pro-American and are likely to remain so.

On the other hand, those nations which are located some distance away from the Communist powers tend to regard the Communist threat as a myth or a "bogey-man" and take refuge in neutralism. In many cases their neutralism takes the form of "benevolent neutralism," which means that they are neutral towards us and benevolent to the other side.

An important example of such a situation is to be found in the present government of Indonesia. As we have already seen, it was in large measure because of American pressure on the Dutch government that the former Dutch East Indies became the independent Indonesian Republic. Since that event the United States has poured vast sums into Indonesia in the form of both economic and military aid, but without achieving any satisfactory results. There are numbers of Indonesians, especially among those inhabiting the outlying islands of Sumatra, Borneo, Celebes, and the Molluccas, who are friendly to the West, but the central government in Java, headed by the dictator Sukarno, is very unfriendly to the United States and openly sympathizes with Communist policies. The only reason that Sukarno does not definitely place his country in the Communist camp is that many of the officers of the Indonesian army are opposed to such a step.

The newly independent states of India, Ceylon, and Burma are firmly committed to neutralism, at least for the time being. Nehru, the dominant figure in Indian politics, both fears and dislikes the United States. Some of his intimate friends, such as Krishna Menon, the Minister of Defense, are even more extreme in their hatred of America. Many sections of the Indian populace feel friendly towards Russia and especially towards Communist China. It should be noted that Communist China's recent aggressiveness has alienated many Hindus and has weakened pro-Communist sympathies. In any case, it is improbable that Nehru will permit India to drift into the Communist camp. Mrs. Bandaranaike, who controls Ceylon, is also adamant in her neutralism. This is unfortunate, since she will permit neither Britain nor the United States to make use of the important naval base of Trincomalee. On the surface, Burma is as rigidly neutralist as the other two countries, but because of the open infiltration and subversion carried out in Burma by the Chinese Communists, it is possible that Burma may eventually be won over to the Western Alliance.

The situation among the Arabic-speaking peoples is somewhat more complicated. A fairly large number of Arabs are friendly to the West in general and to the United States in particular, but such persons are constantly under attack by both the pro-Communists and the extreme followers of the Pan-Arab movement. King Faisal of Iraq and his very able Prime Minister, Nuri-as-said, were extremely friendly to the West and joined the so-called Baghdad Pact. This was the real reason for the violent and bloody revolution in Iraq, ending with the murder of both the King and his Prime Minister. Lebanon for many years was pro-Western, as was also the state of Jordan, but these two states, if they are permitted to survive at all, will probably drift toward neutralism in order to survive internal turmoil.

Colonel Nasser, the dictator of the United Arab Republic (Egypt and Syria), is far from being a Communist. In fact, he is making serious attempts to suppress the Communist movement inside his own domain, but he is violently anti-Western. In spite of the fact that it was the United States which saved him from destruction at the time of the Anglo-French attack, he dislikes the Americans quite as much as the British and the French. He is the militant leader of the Pan-Arab movement, and he believes that the Western powers are the chief obstacles in the path leading to the complete destruction of Israel and the forcible union of all Arabic-speaking peoples into a single state controlled by himself. He is flirting with Russia for Soviet economic and military aid, but if possible, he would like to remain neutral between the free and the Communist worlds.

The Arabic-speaking countries of North Africa to the west of Egypt (Morocco, Tunisia, Libya) are also rapidly drifting towards neutralism. In this case neutralism can seriously injure the strategic position of the Western powers. Extreme nationalists in all of these states are already demanding the elimination of all American air bases in this area. If these demands are refused, the nationalists are likely to attempt to destroy these bases by sabotage.

The situation in Black Africa, Africa south of the Sahara, inhabited mostly by Negroes, is somewhat confused. Only a few states in this area have achieved complete independence, but several other independent Negro republics are certain to be established in the course of the next few years. From present indications, it is almost certain that these states will assume a neutralist position.

Most of the neutralist states are likely to remain neutral and so it is not necessary to make a detailed study of their military capabilities. But because it is *possible* that some or all may be drawn into the limited wars which are likely to take place in the near future, a word or two should be said about the fighting ability of each of these nations.

I do not have a high regard for the armed forces of Indonesia. If they were to be drawn into a military conflict with the Western powers, they would present no serious menace. With guerrilla tactics they could make it difficult to occupy the interior of the big islands, but they would not be strong enough to prevent us, if we so desired, to take a few key bases, such as the great naval base at Surabaya.

In like manner, even if India, Ceylon, and Burma were to join in active hostilities against us, they would not constitute a major danger. In the days of the British Indian army the Sikhs, the Rajputs, and the Mahrattas provided some first-class regiments, but most of the Indian peoples were notoriously lacking in martial tradition. India is much larger than Pakistan and has a far greater population, but from the strictly military point of view, I would rather have the Pakistanis than the Indians as allies. The Singhalese and the Burmese are even less martial than the Indians.

I have already mentioned that I have a rather low opinion of the fighting ability of the modern Arabs, especially of the modern Egyptians. Certainly if we had to choose between the Arabs and the Turks as allies, I would choose the Turks every time. Because of lack of training and equipment, the armed forces of the new Negro states in Africa are likely to be rather ineffective for some time to come.

The Friendly Nations

Finally, we must try to make an estimate of the capabilities and intentions of those nations which are likely to be on our side in case hostilities break out.

It is fairly easy to draw up a list of such states, for we have treaty commitments with nearly all of them. It is true, of course, that a shift in government as the result of a revolution or a popular election might make it necessary to revise this list, but such alterations are not very probable in the immediate future.

We need not go into detail with regard to the nations which together make up NATO. With the possible exception of Iceland, it is probable that all of these nations will live up to their commitments, but there are vast differences with respect to their military capabilities. We can expect little military assistance from such countries as Norway and Denmark. Their most valuable contribution to any war effort would be to grant us permission to use their territory for the creation of our own military bases.

We can expect something more from such nations as The Netherlands and Belgium, but the small size of their population, and hence of their armed forces, makes it impossible for them to become major factors in the defense of Western Europe if Russia attempts an invasion of this area. If war does break out in the West (which I am inclined to doubt), it is certain that the major contributions to the war effort will be made by Great Britain, France, and West Germany.

Great Britain would, no doubt, concentrate on sea and air action, but her army would be of great help in the land defense of the continent of Europe. In France, the coming to power of General de Gaulle has brought about a great increase in national and military morale. As a result, French capabilities are much greater than they were at the beginning of World War II. With respect to purely European defense, France is weakened by the fact that she has to keep so many of her soldiers in North Africa. But in case hostilities start in the Near East, this would be a help rather than a handicap. As regards the land defense of Europe, Germany would be called upon to play a—if not *the*—major role, and I am convinced that she will be able to live up to her responsibilities. The Germans make excellent soldiers, and this time their military ardor would be increased by their desperate desire to keep Germany free from Bolshevik barbarity.

I am sure that Italy will remain true to her treaty obligations, but I seriously doubt that she can render any spectacular military assistance. In fact, I am convinced that Spain (although not a member of NATO) will be of greater help to us than Italy. It is not that I place any great reliance upon the Spanish armed forces, but Spain's geographic position means that *our* bases in that area would be of great assistance in trying to prevent the Russians from marching to the Atlantic Ocean.

The war effort of both Italy and France would be

somewhat handicapped by the fact that a fairly large percentage (about 20 per cent) of the population in both countries would tend to be friendly to the Russian invaders (at least in the early stages). However, the fact that more than 85 per cent of the inhabitants of the satellite countries of Eastern Europe would be violently anti-Russian would more than make up for this weakness.

Turning now from the Atlantic to the Pacific powers, we must note with regret that there is in the Pacific area no overall alliance corresponding to NATO. There is, to be sure, the relatively weak SEATO, which includes the Philippines, South Vietnam, Thailand, and Pakistan. But for political reasons, it was not possible to get South Korea, Japan, Formosa, and Iran into this group, so the United States has been forced to make separate agreements with each of these nations.

In spite of the lack of an overall alliance, I firmly believe that all of the above-named nations will hold firm to their anti-Communist position and will remain in alliance with the United States. In the last few years, anti-American feeling has increased in many of these countries; in fact, there have been sporadic anti-American riots. But as long as these countries need American help to protect themselves from Communist aggression, I do not think that these riots are to be taken very seriously.

A word should be said about the military capabilities of each of these countries. In spite of the absence of military background and tradition, the fighting in Korea shows that (South) Korean soldiers, when properly led, trained, and equipped, make excellent soldiers. Japan's defeat in World War II has considerably weakened her fighting spirit and the new defense force is still far from being the equal of the old Japanese army, but this can be rectified. I confidently expect that if necessary, the Japanese can again turn out a first-class fighting force. The armed forces of Nationalist China are still far from being the best in the world, but they are infinitely better than they were in the 1930's and 1940's. Most of the "rotten apples" (incompetents, grafters, traitors) have been eliminated. The soldiers are better fed, better trained, and better equipped than before. Moreover, their fighting spirit is much improved. The chief drawback of the Nationalist army is the rather high average age of the soldiers, but this situation is being rectified by the recruiting of young Formosan men into the armed forces.

The Filipinos show a marked ability to conduct guerrilla, jungle, and irregular warfare, but because of their lack of training and equipment they would be of less value in a big-scale conflict. The army of South Vietnam has been in existence such a short time that it is impossible to give it a proper evaluation. The personnel look promising, however, and in the course of the next few years may well develop into a crack force. As things are at present, neither the Thai army or navy is of major significance, but it would be well to make use of them as an example of a free Asiatic people voluntarily fighting with us against Communist aggression.

I tend to place a rather high evaluation on the fighting potential of Pakistan, largely because of the fighting spirit of the Pakistanis, especially the West Pakistanis. In the old days of the British Indian army, many of the best regiments were recruited from the Mohammedan inhabitants of the Punjab province which now forms the core of West Pakistan. Even so, Pakistan's army is in sore need of more equipment and better training.

A word must be said about the Turkish armed forces. Technically, Turkey belongs to NATO, but it can best be considered with the other Asiatic nations. I am certain that the Turkish armed forces will give a good account of themselves in the event of war. The Turks are undoubtedly the best fighters in the Near East, and with American equipment they should be able to withstand a Russian invasion.

The armed forces of Iran are not nearly as good as those of Turkey, but their caliber can be greatly improved by the American military mission in that area. Very important, moreover, is the fact that the addition of Iran to the Western Alliance means that Turkey and Pakistan will be linked by a land route, and thus the strategic position of all these countries will be greatly improved.

Brief mention should be made of the armed forces of Israel. Israel will, no doubt, try very hard to preserve her diplomatic neutrality, but if the Arabs, backed by the Russians, assume an actively aggressive position, she will be forced to throw in her lot with the Western powers. If so, the Israeli forces would be a welcome addition to the armed strength of the free world. We know from experience that the modern Israelis make excellent soldiers.

By way of summary, we may say that a careful comparison of the capabilities of the Communist powers, on the one hand, and the free-world powers, on the other, indicates that on balance, the latter have greater potential strength. In fact, it can be said that the free world can definitely defeat the Communist powers in the event of armed conflict *if the free world is willing to make use of its potential strength.*

This means that in order to cope with brush-fire wars, the free world, especially the United States, must maintain an adequate number of combat troops and must also maintain sufficient transport facilities to move these troops to any part of the world on very short notice. It also means that the free world must maintain an adequate number of tactical bombers.

In order to cope with an all-out war, the free world, and, again, especially the United States, must continue its constant research and its testing of ballistic missiles and nuclear bombs. The unilateral abandonment of such research and such testing would be suicidal. It would be almost as disastrous to make an agreement with the Communist powers to a mutual abandonment of ballistic and nuclear research unless the full right of inspection is guaranteed.

In order to cope with either a brush-fire war or an all-out war, we must maintain a firm, vigorous, and positive foreign policy. There are many nations in Europe and Asia which are friendly to us and willing to stand with us in the event of armed conflict. But if we adopt a weak policy and go in for appeasement, their political and military morale will be shattered. They will fear that they will be abandoned in the event of a major crisis and will seek to free themselves from their ties with the United States.

165

7

Grand Strategy
and National Policy

THIS little book has been devoted to a study of strategic intelligence, with hints on how to produce strategic estimates. By way of conclusion, a word should be said about the use which can and should be made of such estimates.

It is obvious that in times of war an estimate of long-term enemy capabilities and intentions is of great value to those in charge of our war plans in aiding them to bring about a victorious peace. In times of peace it is equally important to those in authority to have an esti-mate of when and where and under what circumstances the enemy is likely to commence hostilities against us or any of our allies.

However, in addition to the usefulness of strategic in-telligence in support of ordinary or general strategy, it is also invaluable, if properly used, to those persons, both civilians and military men, who are in charge of what is now called "grand strategy."

Grand strategy has been defined as plans for the use of the political, economic, and psychological powers of a nation, together with its armed forces, during war and during peace, to secure national objectives. Here the em-phasis is on long-term national objectives. To secure these objectives and to preserve them from attack, the state should utilize each means at its disposal. This calls for the close co-ordination of all the governmental agencies involved in dealing with other nations.

The field of grand strategy is so important that we must go into the matter in greater detail, especially since America has devoted so little attention to it in the past. For the most part, the Americans have been rather good at both tactics and strategy, with the result that they have won most of the wars in which they have become involved. But they have been rather poor at grand strategy, and hence their military victories have not always resulted in preserving or augmenting national objectives.

To be more specific, there has frequently been an appalling lack of co-ordination between the various branches of our government with respect to making long-term diplomatic, military, and economic plans. The State Department has frequently erred by formulating diplomatic policies without consultation with the armed services, which policies the armed forces felt they could not implement. In 1931-32, for example, when the Japanese began to march into Manchuria, Mr. Stimson, our Secretary of State, addressed to the Japanese government a series of sharp notes demanding that Japanese troops be withdrawn from this area. We now know that the Japanese made a serious effort to find out if the American armed forces intended to make any attempt to implement these demands before they (the Japanese) made any further commitments. They soon found that our armed forces had no plans for implementation—with the result that after each of Mr. Stimson's notes, the Japanese, instead of moving out, moved farther and farther in, and the United States was made to look ridiculous in the eyes of the world.

In like manner, many of our eminent leaders have also erred in dealing with grand strategy. During World War II, for example, they were busy formulating war plans aiming at the immediate defeat of the enemy, without reference to the long-term effects of these plans upon America's position in the world after the fighting was over. They were so busy trying to crush Hitler, Mussolini, and Tojo that they had no time to consider what was likely to happen to America's position in international politics after these particular enemies had been eliminated.

During World War II, when I served in a very subordinate position with the Joint Chiefs of Staff organization, I was frequently called upon to read and comment on memoranda which the British Joint Chiefs of Staff had sent to our group. In reading these memoranda it became clear to me that in many cases the British Joint Chiefs had consulted with the British Foreign Office before sending them and that the memoranda themselves were an expression of British national policy and not merely the expression of the ideas of the British military leaders. I also became aware that in many cases the American Joint Chiefs answered these memoranda without consulting with the State Department. I also discovered that on many occasions the State Department sent memoranda to the British Foreign Office, memoranda which seriously affected our foreign policy, without prior consultation with the American Joint Chiefs.

This confusion and lack of co-ordination was obvious

to many persons. As a result, in 1945, an attempt was made to improve matters by the formation of SWNCC, or the State, War, Navy Coordinating Committee. This organization fulfilled a very useful function, but it was soon found that its members worked on too low a level to have any decisive influence on national policy. In consequence of this fact, SWNCC was abolished and in its place was established, in 1946, the National Security Council, of which both the Secretary of State and the Secretary of Defense were ex-officio members. This certainly was a step, and a very important step, in the right direction, but for various reasons which I cannot go into here, the National Security Council has never performed quite as efficiently as had been hoped. I sincerely trust that in the next few years the National Security Council will be permitted and required to function more effectively.

Even since the creation of the National Security Council there has been, in my opinion, another weakness in the formulation of our grand strategy. This consists in our making a piecemeal rather than a global approach to many of our problems. We have been in the habit of dealing with a European problem one day, a Near Eastern problem the next day, and a Far Eastern problem the day following without stopping to examine whether or not there is a connection between these problems. It is time that we realize that at present we are dealing with an enemy who does have a global approach to those matters. I am convinced that anything which the Communists do in Korea, in Indochina, in Iraq, or in West Germany is all part and parcel of a single underlying plan. Communist tactics may change from area to area and from time to time, but the basic strategy is the same, and we must be prepared to counteract this strategy.

Basic National Policy

It is agreed that grand strategy is the co-ordinated activity of all government agencies to secure national objectives, but before anything concrete can be accomplished there must be agreement among civilian and military leaders as to what our national objectives are or should be. This agreement can be called the formulation of our basic national policy. Curiously enough, there has been and still is a wide variety of opinions on this point, even among our greatest statesmen.

In this connection it is important that we contrast our position to that of the U.S.S.R. It is clear that ever since 1917, all of the major Soviet leaders have been united in believing that the U.S.S.R. should have not one but two ultimate goals in the conduct of foreign affairs. The first of these goals may be called "territorial aggrandizement" and is centered around the determination that the U.S.S.R. should constantly grow in size and power until in the end it is the supreme power throughout the world. The second goal may be called "ideological aggrandizement" and is centered around the determination of the Soviet leaders that the basic principles of Communism shall be spread until they embrace the whole world. The two goals coalesce in the idea that all the countries of the entire globe, in both the Eastern and Western hemispheres, shall be transformed into a group of nations dominated by Communist hierarchies—and all bound together as satellites of the U.S.S.R.

As I have already indicated, there has never been unanimity as to what the ultimate goal of our foreign policy should be, but at least all of our statesmen have agreed that American foreign policy does not and should not aim at unlimited territorial aggrandizement. During parts of the nineteenth century, to be sure, there were periods when expansionist ideas were popular. We can all call to mind the years when such slogans as "Manifest Destiny" and "54-40 or fight" won widespread popular appeal, but at no time did the Americans even remotely aim at conquering the whole world, and during the twentieth century, they have been aggressively anti-imperialist in attitude. After the Spanish-American War we did indeed annex the Philippines and Puerto Rico, but a few years later we gave complete independence to the Philippines and have solemnly told the Puerto Ricans that they may have their freedom any time they ask for it.

After emerging as victors in two world wars, we could easily have seized large slices of territory in different parts of the world had we wished to do so—but the only expansion we went in for was to secure control over a few scattered islands in the Pacific in order to use them as defense bases in the event of renewed warfare in that area. Because of the violent dislike of territorial aggression by the American people, it is hard for many Americans to understand that unlimited territorial aggrandizement can be and is a basic doctrine among the leaders of the Soviet government.

But whereas all American leaders, whether military or civilian, whether Republican or Democrat, agree in rejecting any form of territorial aggrandizement as a goal for our foreign policy, there is still great difference of opinion as to how far, in our relations with foreign nations, we should aim at the spread of basic American ideologies. Throughout American history there have always been important groups of persons who think that one of the fundamental goals of our foreign policy should be to promote the spread of democratic beliefs and institutions throughout the world.

This feeling was very strong in the years following 1945. There was a strong faction in our government (and more especially in our State Department) which felt that it was our duty to impose a democratic form of government on other nations, even if it necessitated the use of force. This faction was especially vociferous with reference to those countries over which we had a good deal of direct control, such as Italy, Germany, and Japan. This group tried to insist that we should take advantage of our occupation forces in those countries to establish, willy nilly, some sort of a replica of the American form of government.

I have always disagreed, and disagreed rather strongly, with the views of this faction. I am firmly convinced that to be successful, the governmental organization of any nation must be in accord with the cultural and traditional heritage of the nation in question. Hence it is very stupid to try to impose our system of government or our type of economic organization upon a people with an entirely different background who do not share any of our cultural heritage.

In this connection I remember very vividly the bitter battle which was waged in 1945 within governmental circles as to the proper treatment of the Japanese Emperor. There was a powerful group inside our government which insisted that the Emperor be deposed as part of the terms of Japan's surrender or at least that American troops should forcibly establish a republic once we had fully occupied the country. I was one of many who fought this suggestion tooth and nail. It goes without saying that I would be violently opposed to having an "Emperor of the United States," but I was convinced that the long-term interest of America would be better served by permitting the Japanese to preserve the imperial institution. I feel that at the present time most informed Americans would be in accord with this position.

What was true about Japan is also true as regards the other nations of the world. Abstractly, I am still in favor of a republic as opposed to a monarchy, but I do not believe that it should be part of American foreign policy to persuade the British to depose Queen Elizabeth. I am violently opposed to both Fascism and Communism, but I do not believe that American foreign policy should center around the objective of upsetting the Fascist regime of Franco in Spain or the Communist regime of Tito in Yugoslavia as long—but only as long—as these regimes remain friendly and helpful to the United States.

If, then, we reject territorial aggrandizement and ideological aggrandizement as proper goals of American foreign policy, we are brought face to face with this problem: Around what principle should the foreign policy of the United States be centered? To my way of thinking, the answer to this problem is simple: The goal of our foreign policy and of our grand strategy should be, essentially, to protect the integrity and the security of America. We may say that the foreign policy of a President or a Secretary of State and the grand strategy of our military leaders have been successful or unsuccessful according to whether or not they have aided in safeguarding the independence, the security, and the relative strength of the American nation.

Isolationism and Internationalism

We must now approach the much-debated problem of whether the safety and integrity of the United States can best be secured by basing our national policy on the principle of isolationism or on the principle of internationalism. The struggle between the advocates of the two principles began at a very early period in American history and has continued intermittently ever since.

Generally speaking, all throughout the nineteenth century and the early part of the twentieth century, the advocates of isolationism were triumphant. Any suggestion that we contract any "entangling alliances" with a foreign power—even a suggestion that we join in some world conference—was greeted with a howl of dismay by the bulk of the American populace. Even as late as

1917, when we decided to give active support to England and France, Woodrow Wilson thought it necessary to state that the United States was not an "Allied" but only an "associated" power.

And when Wilson tried to make a sharp break with the isolationist tradition by demanding that America join the newly constituted League of Nations, this led to a long and bitter discussion in Congress and among the American people. For the time being, the isolationist tradition had triumphed, and the United States refused to join the League of Nations or even the World Court.

During the latter part of World War II, however, there was a sharp reversal of public sentiment. President Roosevelt, by means of a series of very astute political moves, was able to convert a large number of Senators and Congressmen to the idea that the United States should join the United Nations. More important still, he was able to convert the bulk of the American people to the same way of thinking. Almost overnight, isolationism became a term of opprobrium, and both Democrats and Republicans embraced the new gospel of collective security.

Many of the new converts were wildly optimistic in their appraisal of what the United Nations could be expected to accomplish. Under the aegis of the United Nations, imperialism and power politics were to be forever abolished; international understanding and perpetual peace were to be established almost automatically. The widespread acceptance of this line of thought had a marked effect upon our defense program. Many persons sincerely believed that with the United Nations in operation, there was little or no need to keep up a large army, navy, or air force.

The events of the last few years have disillusioned many of these naïve optimists. We have seen that the United Nations, for all its virtues, is not an infallible cure for all of the evils of the world. We have seen that it does not automatically secure peace or guarantee our national security. As a result, there has been a marked change in public sentiment. I am convinced that the majority of the American people are still in favor of some kind of collective security, but in many places we can witness the revival of the old isolationist—or at least a semi-isolationist—point of view.

I personally think that the extreme advocates of isolationism and the extreme advocates of internationalism are both wrong. I am of the opinion that we Americans should be neither isolationist nor internationalist but, rather, nationalist in our approach to world problems. Isolationism must be rejected because it is absurd to say that American security would not be affected by the turn of events in Europe and Asia. From a purely selfish point of view, we must be vitally concerned with whether or not the free countries in other parts of the world are able to maintain themselves against the Red menace.

At the same time, naïve internationalism must be rejected, since it, too, threatens American security. I do not believe that the goal of American foreign policy should be to establish world government. At the present stage of civilization, world government is impractical, and even if it were possible, it would be deeply injurious to our standard of living and to the American way of life. I am of the opinion that we should work with and for the United Nations, but only to the extent that such a line of action helps to maintain American security and integrity.

Moreover, we must be realistic about what the United Nations can and cannot accomplish. This means that we must be in a position to maintain our security in case the United Nations collapses. If we had merely relied on the United Nations to repel invasion, Korea would certainly have been lost to the free world. We cannot afford to be isolationist, but we must be internationalist only to the extent that our commitments to other nations, singly and collectively, promote the welfare of the United States.

The United States, to protect its security, must take an intelligent interest in the political and military developments in all parts of the world, even in areas which are only of indirect concern to us. But there are five areas which are of immediate and vital concern to us. Our foreign policy and its implementation, our grand strategy, must take careful and continuing interest in these areas, lest American security be undermined.

The first of these areas contains the countries of the Western Hemisphere. I am certain that most Americans would agree that all the countries of both North and South America must be protected against any possible aggression from outside, whether this aggression takes the form of overt invasion or of internal subversion by foreign agents. This means, of course, that we must maintain the spirit of the old Monroe Doctrine, with suitable modifications to suit present-day conditions.

The second and third areas consist of what are usually called the Far East and Southeast Asia. If at any time in the foreseeable future any unfriendly power or group of powers should secure control over these two areas, America's position in the world would be seriously endangered and we would be forced into a major war to protect our interests. In order to avert such a calamity, we must establish and maintain a new Open Door Policy to take the place of the old Open Door Policy, which collapsed because of our ruinous inaction at a time of crisis.

The fourth and fifth areas are generally called Western Europe and the Near East. It is generally agreed that if the whole or even any major part of Western Europe were threatened by a power or a group of powers unfriendly to ourselves, the outbreak of World War III would be inevitable. To avert this disaster, we must continue to build up and strengthen such agencies as NATO. Perhaps it would be better to say that we must establish an Open Door Policy for Western Europe.

The Near East is not of such vital importance as Western Europe, but because of the oil situation and also because this area is the gateway to Africa, every effort must be made to see that the Near East, at least as a whole, does not come under Communist control. Perhaps this can best be done by a revival of the now moribund Baghdad Pact.

Let us now make a brief analysis of the problems we face and the policies to be carried out in each of these areas.

The Monroe Doctrine

First, with regard to the Western Hemisphere and the Monroe Doctrine, everyone knows that the Monroe Doctrine gets its name because of President Monroe's allusion to its principles in a message to Congress in 1823. Comparatively few persons seem to realize that the original proposal which led to the formulation of the doctrine came from George Canning, the British Foreign Minister at that time. Canning was aware that Spain, with the backing of the major Continental powers, was thinking about making an earnest effort to recover her colonies in Latin America. He also realized that if the effort succeeded it would be a serious blow to British interests in that area.

For this reason he proposed to the United States the formation of an Anglo-American alliance aimed at maintaining Latin American independence. This proposal was given serious consideration in the United States, and several persons spoke in favor of accepting it. It was John Quincy Adams, the Secretary of State, who conceived the notion that America would secure even greater benefits by making a unilateral declaration of policy, knowing that England would be forced by circumstances to back up this policy.

Following Adams' suggestion, President Monroe announced to the world that the United States would look with extreme displeasure upon any attempt by a European power to conquer or to reconquer any portion of the Western Hemisphere. This was all very fine, but let us never forget that at this time we had no army and no navy worthy of the name. If we had had to rely only upon our own forces, we could not possibly have enforced the new policy in the event that the European powers made a serious move in opposition to it. But Adams proved right in his prediction that the British would feel compelled to back it up—and at that time Britain still ruled the waves. For the next few decades the Monroe Doctrine was a success, but only because we could induce the British, for their own selfish reasons, to pull our chestnuts out of the fire.

Originally, the Monroe Doctrine was in fact, if not in theory, merely a warning to the Spanish, the French, and the Russians that they should keep out of the Western World. It was not until 1895, more than seventy years after the Doctrine was first announced to the world, that the United States, with greatly augmented naval forces, felt strong enough to apply the Doctrine to the British as well when the latter attempted to intervene in Venezuela. Since that time the Monroe Doctrine has succeeded very well, but only because we have been tenacious in our intention to maintain it and have had the military force necessary to keep it in operation.

There can be no doubt that the Latin American nations have benefited greatly from the Monroe Doctrine. It is because of the Doctrine that these nations have maintained their independence and their territorial integrity. But it is certain that for a long period the Monroe Doctrine was extremely unpopular among the nations it benefited. They felt that the very existence of the Doctrine placed them in an inferior and humiliating position with reference to the "Colossus of the North."

They were especially resentful that under Theodore Roosevelt and his successors the Monroe Doctrine was used as an excuse to intervene in the internal affairs of the smaller Latin American countries. Roosevelt took the position that if the United States assumed the responsibility of protecting the Latin American countries from European aggression, she was morally bound to see that these nations paid their just debts and carried out their other obligations to the European powers, even if it meant armed intervention by American troops.

There was much to be said for this position, but it aroused much passionate opposition south of the Rio Grande, and a great many Latin Americans regarded the whole Monroe Doctrine as a mask for Yankee imperialism.

This situation has been radically altered, and altered for the better, by developments which took place after World War I, particularly during the administrations of Franklin D. Roosevelt and his successors in the White House. As a result of the Treaty of Chapultepec in 1945 and the Treaty of Rio de Janeiro in 1948, the Monroe Doctrine received new and important modifications. It is no longer a unilateral expression on the part of the United States of her intention to defend the Western Hemisphere from external attack. It is now a multilateral expression by all of the American nations of their willingness to aid one another in the event of a threat to any one of them by an Old World power.

I am of the opinion that this reinterpretation has had very valuable results. It remains true, of course, that the United States is the strongest and the most influential of the American republics. In the event of a threat to the Western Hemisphere, the defense of this area will depend in large measure on the armed forces of the United States. For psychological reasons, however, it is far better to say that we are ready to defend Brazil from attack

181

because Brazil has promised to defend us from attack, or even that we will guarantee the independence of Costa Rica because Costa Rica has promised us to help in maintaining our independence. Our foreign policy should be realistic, but realism includes an appreciation of the sensitivity of our potential allies.

I also think that it was very wise to renounce, as a general principle, the right to intervene unilaterally in the domestic affairs of our Latin American neighbors, if only because of the effect of this renunciation on Latin American public opinion. There are some of our political leaders who wish to go back to intervention, at least to the extent that they wish to have our government actively co-operate with revolutionary movements in those Latin American countries which seek to overthrow dictators. Such a policy would be both stupid and dangerous.

I have already pointed out that for a governmental organization to succeed it must be in accord with the cultural and traditional heritage of the nation in question. In some of the Latin American nations, the people are not yet ready for *real* democracy and a quasi-dictatorship is the only way in which stability can be maintained. Moreover, as Representative Jackson has pointed out, "the history of Latin America is replete with instances of revolution against one man rule which resulted, not in easing the plight of the people, but in the installation of another strong man and an equally repugnant dictatorship under another name."

In general, then, it is advisable to maintain the policy of non-intervention, but in one instance intervention may not only be advisable but necessary. This is when, by force or fraud, the Communists take over the government of any Latin American country. The Russians are not likely to launch an overt military attack upon Latin America, but, following their favorite policy of infiltration and subversion, they may well be able to establish a popular-front government which is later transformed into an outright Communist dictatorship. Such a step would be as serious a blow at the Monroe Doctrine as an armed invasion, and the United States must act promptly and forcibly—preferably in close connection with the Organization of American States, all of whose members are pledged to support "the effective exercise of representative democracy."

The Open Door Policy in Asia

Let us now turn to an examination of the Open Door Policy, the part it has played in determining our relations with other powers, and how it can best be re-established and maintained in the future.

In some ways we can say that the Open Door Policy is very old, dating back to our first contacts with the countries of the Far East. If we study what the United States did and did not do in China during the period of the First and Second Opium wars, we will find that the Americans had already tacitly adopted the policy which was later called the Open Door Policy. In like manner, what Commodore Perry and Townsend Harris aimed at in Japan during the period 1853-1858 was also in loose accord with this same policy.

But the Open Door Policy in its final and explicit form dates back only to 1899-1900, when John Hay was Secretary of State. In 1899, we had just emerged from the Spanish American War and as a result of that war had secured possession of the Philippines. For some decades previously we had not been greatly concerned with developments in the Far East, but because of our recently acquired foothold in the Philippines, the American public and the Department of State became acutely interested in what was happening in China. We discovered, to our amazement, that the ancient Chinese Empire was being threatened with imminent collapse.

The Sino-Japanese War of 1894-1895, from which Japan emerged as an easy victor, showed that China, far from being a "sleeping dragon," was weak and powerless. Many of the great powers of the world decided to take advantage of the situation. They extracted valuable concessions from the Manchu rulers of China and also demanded—and secured—recognition of special "spheres of influence." The Russians secured recognition of the principle that all of the Chinese Empire north of the Great Wall was to be part of the Russian sphere of influence. The Germans secured complete control of the port of Tsingtao and recognition that the whole of the province of Shantung was to form part of the German sphere of influence. The French secured complete control of the port of Kwang-chou-wan in Southern China and recognition of a French sphere of influence in a large portion of Southwest China. The Japanese made a formal claim that the province of Fukien, facing the island of Formosa, should be considered their sphere of influence.

At first the British were opposed to the idea that China should be split up into a number of spheres of influence for the very good reason that such a division interfered with the normal flow of British goods into all parts of China, but when it appeared that the other powers were going to be successful in their demands for special spheres of influence, the British, too, demanded a special sphere which was to embrace the whole of the Yangtse Valley. To most students of international affairs, it appeared that the Chinese Empire was headed for complete collapse, to be followed by the partition of the Empire between Japan and the great powers of Europe.

It was just at this time that Hay decided to take action. After lengthy consultations with a number of experts on the Far East, both American and British, he proceeded to propound the Open Door Policy as being in the best interests of China, the United States, and the world in general. The Open Door Policy demanded that in China there should be "special privilege for none; equal opportunity for all" and also that the territorial integrity of China should be respected. The plea for "special privilege for none; equal opportunity for all" meant, of course, that the United States made no demands for special rights and privileges but did demand that all the rights and privileges granted to other foreigners be shared by American citizens. The plea for the territorial integrity of China meant that the political, military, and economic independence of China should be respected by all the powers.

In 1899, and again in 1900, Hay sent notes to all of the major powers, pleading for the general recognition of the Open Door Policy. The Japanese, the Russians, the Germans, and the French were distinctly cool toward the proposal, though none of them felt in a position openly to attack or defy the idea. The British, on the other hand, after a little hesitation, accepted the proposal with enthusiasm, and it was because of this fact that the Open Door Policy operated successfully for several years. Most Americans are proud, and justly proud, of the role which the United States played in the formulation of the Open Door Policy—but they are apt to forget that it worked well only as long as there was force to back it up. It operated smoothly from 1900 to 1914, largely because in addition to our own Far Eastern squadron there was also a British fleet off the China coast which stood ready to give support in case of need.

The Open Door Policy began to weaken towards the close of 1914, when the British had to withdraw their naval vessels in order to make use of them in the fight against Germany. During the period 1915-1918, Japan took advantage of the situation and sought to secure predominant power in China by means of the Twenty-one Demands, and it looked for a while as if the Open Door Policy might be permanently wrecked.

The collapse of Germany in 1918 brought about the temporary revival of the Open Door Policy. The American and British navies were once more free to take decisive action in case of trouble in the Far East. The more extreme of the Japanese demands on China were withdrawn and at the Washington Conference of 1922, provision was made for the complete restoration of the Open Door Policy. In fact, in the treaties drawn up at the Conference, the principles of the Open Door Policy were, for the first time, specifically recognized and accepted by the major powers.

All of this was well and good, and the American public sat back in a state of complacent optimism. Only a few years later, however, Japan kicked over the traces and again began a series of aggressive actions. These were begun in 1932 with the Manchurian Incident and were continued in 1935 with an overt action to control North China which in 1937 was developed into an attempt to secure control of the whole of the Chinese Republic. From the beginning the United States made a desperate effort to stem the tide and appealed to England for support. This time, however, Britain refused to come to our assistance because she had already embarked on a policy of trying to appease the aggressor powers, and it looked as if the Open Door Policy was again on the verge of collapse.

Notwithstanding this situation, the United States was determined not to abandon her time-honored policy, and this very fact was the cause of our war with Japan. It was because America insisted that Japan withdraw her troops from China and restore the Open Door Policy that the Japanese made their attack on Pearl Harbor, with results that are known to all of us. In our campaign against Japan, we spent many billions of dollars and we lost many hundreds of thousands of young men as casualties. For a while it looked as if all of these sacrifices were worth while. The Japanese surrendered in 1945, and it was taken for granted that the Open Door Policy would be automatically restored.

We were soon to be bitterly disillusioned. Because of our foolishness in disregarding the Communist menace, the situation is now far worse than it was in December, 1941. In China today there is special privilege for one power only, and that an enemy power. There is equal opportunity for no other power, neither for ourselves nor for the English, who have been foolish enough to try and curry favor by appeasement. The Open Door Policy has received a smashing blow, and I foresee a great deal of trouble for the United States before this policy is restored once more.

For the moment, at least, it is not possible to re-establish the old Open Door Policy as regards continental China. This very fact means that we must establish and maintain a new Open Door Policy with respect to the other parts of the Far East and Southeast Asia. If the Chinese Communists succeed in overrunning these areas, America's position in world affairs will be seriously injured; hence the necessity of maintaining close military alliances with South Korea, Japan, and Formosa, as well as with such countries as the Philippines, Vietnam, and Thailand.

It is also imperative that we continue to refuse to grant legal recognition to Red China or permit her to enter the United Nations and the Security Council, at least as long as the Chinese Communists retain their present aggressive policy. To grant legal recognition at the present time would give us no advantage. Any agreements made with the Chinese Communists are not worth the paper they are written on (as we know from the Korean Armistice Agreement). Recognition would greatly weaken our allies in the other parts of the Far East, and they would regard such action as a betrayal of their interests. It would practically force the large Chinese minority in Southeast Asia to embrace Communism in order to survive. In addition, there is at present serious and widespread unrest inside Communist China, which may well lead, before long, to open revolution. Granting recognition at this stage would greatly weaken the morale of the actual and potential rebels and enormously strengthen the position of the Communist hierarchy over the mass of the Chinese people.

The Open Door Policy in Western Europe and in the Near East

It has been only during the last few decades that we have felt forced to intervene in European affairs. At the time of the Napoleonic Wars, we were far too weak to take sides in the struggle for the control of Europe. From 1815 to 1914, there was no need for us to intervene in European matters, for during this period the balance of power between the great European nations was such that no one nation could overrun the whole of Western Europe and hence imperil our own position in world affairs.

Whether we were justified in entering World War I is still a matter of argument, even among experts, but the very fact that we did so was a sign that the American people believed that it was disadvantageous to let a single power, such as Germany, dominate the Continent. The same attitude was an important factor in making the American public accept our entry into World War II.

Our grand strategy was seriously at fault when we failed to see that with Germany overwhelmingly defeated, Soviet Russia would certainly attempt to bring the whole of Europe under her sway. Our leaders only became aware of this situation about the middle of 1947, and since then every effort has been made to bolster the free countries against a possible attack by the Russian Communists. Financial aid has been given through the Marshall Plan and military assistance through the formation of the North Atlantic Treaty Organization.

For the future, financial aid can well be tapered off, and at a fairly rapid rate, but the North Atlantic Treaty Organization must be continued and strengthened. In this connection it might be well for the President or Congress to formulate what might be called the Open Door Policy for Western Europe—that it is and will be a fixed American policy to preserve the territorial integrity of free Europe, in which there will be equal opportunity for all and special privilege for none.

If we are and must be committed to maintain a free Western Europe, it follows as a consequence that we are and must be committed to maintain an Open Door Policy in the Near East, for, as we have seen, Western Europe cannot maintain its military power without access to the oil fields of the Near East. Any threat by an unfriendly power to seize the whole of this area or to stop the flow of oil to the West must be met with diplomatic action if possible or with armed force if necessary.